THE MOON IN THE BANYAN TREE

THE MOON IN THE BANYAN TREE

Gael Harrison

ATHENA PRESS
LONDON

THE MOON IN THE BANYAN TREE
Copyright © Gael Harrison 2005

ISBN 1 84401 481 9

First Published 2005 by
ATHENA PRESS
Queen's House, 2 Holly Road
Twickenham, TW1 4EG
United Kingdom

Printed for Athena Press

For Gerry, who was my lifeline whilst I was in Tien Yen and John, who made sense of all my scribblings.

Balcony, Hang Gai Street, Hanoi, Vietnam
July 2002

It has only been a week and I am so out of sorts, hot and sticky with swollen fingers and ankles. I wonder if I will ever fit any of my shoes again, and my feet look like a battleground of Elastoplast.

I have just come back from Edinburgh where I have been for six weeks' holiday. I said goodbye again to the mountains, the wet pavements and all my loved ones. Apart from pangs of homesickness, I am readjusting to my new Vietnam experiences and am impatient to get my body back to normal. It is difficult racing around buying cutlery, plates and pillows when the heat is suffocating and the sweat runs like rivers, unchecked as arms and hands are laden with parcels. Jungles should evoke this type of imagery, but I am in this concrete world of fumes and pollution, where mosquitoes, rats and cockroaches are still very much in evidence. I am just so hot and the humidity is like an unseen curtain of dampness that will not lift. When will I readjust?

Last night I went out to eat dinner and visited my favourite pavement restaurant near the railway station. There were no tablecloths or candles or little dishes of olives or sophisticated people in fashionable clothes. The menu was a wooden board stuck on a nail on the street wall. It offered two choices: mee soup with pork; or mee soup with fish dumplings. For VND 5,000 (Vietnamese dong) – about 25p – I was served a giant bowl of noodles, pork, peanuts and half a year's supply of greenery floating in a spicy stock. I sat alone, the only foreigner amongst Vietnamese families. The child-size tables were blue and plastic, and the stools were about six inches off the pavement; all around were the remains of the last occupant's meal – soiled napkins, bits of gristle and discarded tooth picks. Containers of chopsticks, sauces and paper napkins were passed around from table to table. In all there were about five tables, and newcomers were not sent away, but instead another stool was brought and they happily joined an existing group of diners.

As I ate, I watched the female chef sitting about two metres from me, presiding over two charcoal burners. On a table in front of her she had about twenty dishes of ingredients that she casually spooned into bowls ready to be covered with the hot soup. It was all very methodical, and steam billowed up as she slammed lids on and off. Her kitchen was the pavement; the street walls were filthy and the drains were piled with the day's rubbish. Masked ladies wearing long gloves would collect it all later and pile it into carts that they pulled around the city, ringing a bell as though they were heralding the old call for leprosy: 'Unclean, unclean.' By ten o'clock at night, the streets would be free of trash and the rats would have a hard time finding anything in the gutters.

The sun was a red ball as it sat on top of the blackening rooftops; night was falling and I relished my meal. Two ladies joined me and we smiled. They asked me my name, how old I was, and where I came from – standard questions when meeting anyone new in Vietnam. I told them I was a teacher; they told me they were gynaecologists. When we had finished our meal, they paid my bill and offered me a lift home on their motorbike. We all squashed on and, as we weaved through the traffic, I had to reflect that the open generosity shown to me time and time again in Vietnam is more than the wide smile that is so freely given; it is the warmth and care and spontaneous friendship that is offered so abundantly. It is this that makes foreigners feel so welcome. I knew then I was happy to be back.

Vietnam in July

I lean over my balcony in Hang Gai Street and watch the constant flow of mayhem beneath me. *Xe oms* by the hundred race past. These are the motorbike taxis that are the main form of public transport. In Vietnamese, *xe may* is motorbike, and *om* is to cuddle, so it is all very literal and reassuring as you hang on to your driver as he negotiates through the traffic to get you to your destination. The fear factor comes in when he tries to do this much quicker than anyone else.

Along with the *xe oms* there are bicycles, cyclos and street vendors carrying mobile markets balanced on their shoulder poles. So much noise, colour, variety; and everyone seems to have such purpose. As I watch I wonder where they are all going, and do they ever get there, and don't they ever stop? So many horns, so much impatience.

I am in my new apartment, right in the heart of the old quarter of Hanoi. My landlord is an octogenarian called Mr Phuong, and I share the building and staircase with all his family. I live on the second floor, and it all becomes quite intimate as I pass through their living areas, on rickety stairs that cut through and round another family's home, and see people preparing food or hanging out washing. A faded parade of intimate personal garments hang like worn-out flags along the stairway and on the balconies. New Year decorations of gold and silver tinsel are still draped around the many pot plants on the stairs; they make me smile as I return after my trips to gather things to feather my little nest, which sits up above this warren of humanity.

The whole jumble of apartments reminds me of a private village, with all the generations living side by side. Slowly I am getting to recognise sons and daughters and grandchildren. Being a foreigner I am allowed certain idiosyncrasies; I am also granted some privacy, and on the whole I am left alone, although of course there is the constant curiosity about my daily comings and goings. Like most people I need quiet and peace and a time to shut out the world, and this apartment does give me that, but I miss the freedom to come and go without anyone noticing. Security is tight here, and we have to padlock iron grilles each time we go in or out; one for the street, then one for the stairs and finally the key to our own homes. It does kill the spontaneity of running out to buy bread, knowing that you have to open the great clanking gates of the prison each time.

Yesterday I bought a painting, and as I write the girl in the frame is watching me. She is exquisite. Dressed in a red cheongsam, the traditional Chinese dress, she looks pensive as she prepares for her wedding. She sits against a black background on a red silk patterned bed cover. On the opposite side of the room, my bed is covered by the quilt I made during my first year in Vietnam. It is sewn from three shades of green silk cut into hexagon shapes, and was stitched patiently over six months. It was supposed to symbolise the greens of the rice fields and the peacefulness of the rural scenery. On the wall above is an embroidered picture of a lotus pond. In such a short time I have created a room that I shall want to live in and return to. It will be the first home that I have ever lived in that will be mine and mine alone.

It is dark and only the jagged forks of lightning illuminate the sky. I have lifted all my pot plants out so that they will get a good soaking when the rain does come. Two special pots have pride of place. These hold the baby trees that I planted in spring this year in Tien Yen. They were the seeds from a tree with beautiful flowers that greeted the morning all silvery white, then as the day grew warmer they turned pink, and finally blushed a deep red when the sun was at its hottest. As evening came they turned white once more. No doubt they have a name, and no doubt someone will tell me...

I was told that, as a foreigner living in Vietnam, I should plant a tree or bush; it would be time for me to leave the country only after my plant had flowered or given fruit. I don't know how the Immigration Department would feel about that. In the meantime my trees are loved and nurtured and I watch them grow.

Sitting here, watching the forked lightning and seeing the street across from me light up in a complicated jumble of roofs and extensions, I want to feel optimistic about the year ahead. I believe that having a positive attitude can colour the outlook to a day or a month or a year, and generally I do try to see things through spectacles that may be tinged with rose-coloured glass. In spite of this, I am afraid of optimism for optimism's sake, and can see how naïve it would be to search for an Eldorado or the Best of All Possible Worlds.

I re-read Voltaire's *Candide* this summer, and tried to remember the optimism that kept me going all of last year. I remember smiling at the ludicrous story line and the irrepressible Pangloss, but took my glasses off and stopped reading as I considered the ultimate message that was delivered to Candide: 'Go and cultivate a garden.' He was advised that the effort would promote activity, self-support and production, and if he developed and cultivated his own talents and harmonised what he wanted with what the rest of society wanted then he could take responsibility for his own happiness. I thought about it and realised that there was a relevance and truth that I could apply to my own life. Perhaps I should put aside my rose-tinted glasses and face my new life with confidence. Wise words, but difficult for such a hardcore romantic optimist to maintain.

My new life began in February 2001. I sat at my computer in Edinburgh and applied to be a volunteer with VSO (Volunteer Services Overseas). I was sad; a love affair wasn't working out and the prospect of the same routines going on for innumerable years seemed so futile. Surely I had something worthwhile that I could contribute elsewhere in return for the experience of living in another culture whilst I was fit and healthy? Great snowflakes were falling on the old city tenements when I pressed 'send' for my application; I had no idea what I had actually set in motion for myself.

The selection interview in London was followed by preparation weekends at Harbourne Hall in Birmingham. Though I didn't yet know where I would be sent, I was swept along. Spring turned into summer and I remember walking through the beautiful old graveyard next to Harbourne Hall looking at bluebells and inscriptions and not really relating to all this new information.

I was still teaching in Stockbridge Primary School in Edinburgh and my new adventure was a talking point. I heard myself spout clichéd phrases like 'My children have grown up, and being divorced I have no real ties', and 'It seems to be the right time to do this', and 'It will be a challenge and who knows... I may help to make a difference in some small way'. They were all just words, and as I reassured my parents and children, perhaps I was really reassuring myself.

The letter arrived telling me I was to be sent to Vietnam.

Although I had spent my early childhood in Malaysia and then nine of my married years in Singapore and Kota Kinabalu in Sabah, East Malaysia (or as it used to be known, North Borneo), I knew very little about Vietnam. I had seen the TV footage and press photographs depicting the horrors of the Vietnam War, and when my husband Dave and I lived in Singapore we were close to Bob, Roger and

Gordon, American GIs who had left Vietnam after the fall of Saigon in 1975. We used to sit on our veranda in the house at Changi, drinking beer and tequila, and they would tell us what it was like trying to adjust to living in a peaceful Asian city after their experiences in the US Army, fighting in Vietnam. They had become commercial divers on their return to the US and had been sent to Singapore in 1976, where they worked on the dive support vessels for the oil fields and exploration sites of Burma, Indonesia, and in the Bay of Bengal.

I remembered black velvet nights, hibiscus, bougainvillaea and frangipani, and I somehow imagined that Vietnam would be the same and the people similar to the gentle Malays and the no-nonsense, efficient Chinese. I would learn that, as in Europe, each nation has been marked by its own history and the people reflect their own way of life. Asia as a whole seems like a beautiful rainbow; each country is made up of its own unique colours, which are reflected in the food, clothes, language and culture. And Vietnam is Vietnam.

The months leading up to departure saw my arm turn into a pincushion for exotic diseases. I tried to read everything I could about the country, but the information was often dry and far too 'textbook'. I was not prepared for the actuality that hit me on my arrival... the geography, history, culture and traditions struck me as a tremendous symphony of colour and sound.

On a map, Vietnam is an S-shaped serpent that slithers down from China, silent as any sleeping dragon, but with the same fearsome potential of blowing great puffs of fire when attacked. Its eastern coastline runs for 3,451 kilometres and has sunlit beaches washed by the waters of the Gulf of Tonkin in the north and the South China Sea to the south. Inland, away from the exotic coastline, runs a spine of great forested mountains in hues of dark, rich greens. Great rivers cut through the landmass, from the mountains of Yunun Province in South West China to the delta of the Red River in the north and the Mekong in the south. Water is a huge problem and thirty years of war have played havoc with the sewerage systems; houses in the cities of Hanoi and Ho Chi Minh have been rebuilt on top of rubble with little thought given to basic drainage requirements.

Through the centuries the Red River has changed its course several times, leaving lakes and ponds in Hanoi that serve as natural outfalls for rainwater. However, the massive deluges caused by the monsoon act as forces of disaster, damaging dykes and resulting in destruction of crops, animals, housing and human life. The dyke building in Vietnam began in the twelfth century and the network, about three thousand kilometres long, stretches across most of the country. These dykes may be as much as fourteen metres high and challenge the Great Wall of China and the Egyptian Pyramids with the sheer volume of earthwork involved. Much can be lost in the catastrophe of colossal rainfall, and it is a fine balance to keep life safe and water controlled in this land where life is dependent on rice and all vegetation exudes moisture and wetness.

In the south, the mighty Mekong finally reaches the sea after its journey through all of Vietnam's neighbours. This river runs like poetry through the exotic lands of a classroom atlas. It starts its 4,400 kilometre course high in the Himalayas and meanders through Myanmar, Laos, Thailand and Cambodia before finally flowing through Vietnam and into the waters of the South China Sea. It is responsible for creating the entire delta region through the slow build up of silt deposits, enabling the soaring production of 'white gold', as farmers call their rice. But each year from May to October the monsoon brings flooding, with the predictable but catastrophic loss of life and infrastructure.

In the north, huge rock formations jut out of the earth and sea in huge single monoliths. Tiny man-made vessels of nailed wood and sail float past these magnificent creations; people are minimised and insignificant in the watery tableau as the great limestone rocks rise up with no beach or landing places, and only the sea eagles have access to the rocky precipices looming above. Three thousand of these islands make up Halong Bay, one of Vietnam's most famous tourist attractions and now a World Heritage Site. Thousands of visitors come and are enchanted by the amazing phenomena of these stone towers, the gaping caverns and grottos that are hidden behind lianas and creepers, all reminiscent of a child's adventure story.

I was told that I would be working for SCF (Save the Children Fund (UK)) as a Preschool Teacher Trainer. My job was to assist teachers to teach Vietnamese as a second language in Quang Ninh Province, northeast of Hanoi. This area of Vietnam is inhabited by a number of ethnic minority groups, who are among the poorest in Vietnam. In the villages where I would be working there are mainly Dao, as well as San Chi minorities. The Dao belong to the Dao-Hmong language group and they, together with the Hmong, are normally living at the highest elevations among the different ethnic groups in Vietnam. Both groups arrived in Vietnam from China in the eighteenth and nineteenth centuries. The language of the San Chi group is a Han language, or a Chinese-based one.

Since graduating as a teacher in 1975 from Dundee College of Education, I had worked in Singapore, Kota Kinabalu and then in the Highlands of Scotland. For the last eight years I had been in Edinburgh. I was full of doubts about my ability to train teachers in another language; I was full of doubts about my ability to live in an isolated part of Vietnam; I was just full of doubts.

British Airways allowed me twenty-three kilogrammes

of luggage, so I squashed fleeces for the cold weather, cotton shirts for the boiling summers, mosquito spray, school books, a short-wave radio and twelve packets of hair dye with colours ranging from Oslo to Helsinki! I suppose each person had their own particular luxury item that they felt they could not live without. For me, there was no way that I was going to go *au naturel*. I also packed a large, blank diary; I wondered how it would look after all my adventures!

Hanoi, 20 August 2001

My dearest Gerry,

I have been talking to you all the time in my head, telling you everything. It is all so hot and so humid. Yesterday I went eleven hours without going to the toilet, I was so busy sweating. The flight was fine, the wait in Bangkok long and tiring, and the arrival in Hanoi a blur of heat and new impressions. The immigration processing was slow, and we had time to read a large sign over the Passport Control booth: DO NOT BRING HUMAN ASHES THIS WAY. Clare, another new volunteer, and I just looked at each other and raised our eyebrows in a very James Bond sort of way.

VSO mixed up the time of our arrival and there was nobody to meet us, so we took a taxi into town. The rice fields and conical hats and buffalo were so beautiful I had a lump in my throat, but the heat was a shock.

We booked into a hotel in the old part of the city; bikes, people, fruit, noise, smells – our senses were on overdrive. Our rooms were on the fourth floor, so we had a long climb up the stairs carrying those heavy cases. We went out for a meal and, after turning down one restaurant that specialised in 'mixed dried blood' and meat that 'was raw or half raw', we found a more civilised one that was good – it had a table cloth!

We slept like logs, then in the morning VSO found us, we moved to our current hotel (also on the fourth floor), and we had an orientation of the city in cyclos (similar to the trishaws of Malaysia). There don't seem to be any traffic rules, and everything just moves in great waves. No one looks right or left; in fact no one really looks at all. The responsibility seems to be hierarchical: the bicycle gives way to the pedestrian; the motorbike to the bicycle; and the car to the motorbike and so on until you get to the lorry or the bus.

Today we started our Vietnamese language classes. They are so hard, and all the sounds are made through the nose and dip ever so

17

slightly up or down, which of course changes the meaning. The Vietnamese are supposed to have a wonderful sense of humour, and I suppose it's no wonder as the chance for puns and the play on words can turn a simple sentence into one full of sexual innuendo. There is a lot of hilarity when a foreigner makes an attempt, as one word can have maybe five different meanings, depending on the intonation used.

Our group is going to Halong Bay this weekend, so that should be fun. They are nice people, six of us altogether. Clare is an English Teacher going to work in a National Park in the centre of Vietnam; Emma is going to teach English at a Teacher's Training College in Da Lat. She will be there with a Dutch lad, Arijan, who will be working with the Forestry. There is Chad, a Canadian who will be teaching English at a National Park in Vinh, and Chris will be in the northwest in Sapa as a Teacher Trainer. Anyway, our trip to Halong Bay will be good for 'bonding'.

It is the heat and humidity that are getting to me, I wonder if I shall ever get used to it?

I was so upset leaving you in Edinburgh and howled all the way to London. I can still see your face when I came in at night and you gave me your presents. I just wanted to hug and hug you, but you will be fine, and soon the house will have your 'stamp' on it and you will make it your own.

Till the next time, I miss you,
Love Mum

Hanoi, 26 August 2001

Hello, hello, hello,

Well how are you, and all the administration in the flat? How are my cats and fish, and the carpets? Are they clean? And are you taking pride in your sink? I just hope so.

Lessons are going well, and now I know some vocabulary and can buy stuff and am learning the money. Food is an experience; we eat all these strange dishes, and drink a lot of beer, and then split the bill. Last night I think I paid a pound! When you ask if someone slept well, you say did you sleep deliciously? Ngu Ngon!

I went to the Save the Children offices and met my new colleagues. They all seem very friendly and efficient and made me feel very welcome. Their names are so unusual – very short, with only one syllable, so hopefully they will be easy to learn.

I am still coping, though the humidity is awful. I was nearly sick with the stench of raw meat, offal and blood in the market; I don't think I want to have to do my food shopping there.

Love Mum

Hanoi, 28 August 2001

Dear Gerry,

Loved Halong Bay. Sat on the boat for three hours watching all these amazing mountains rise out of the sea, in my Gucci sunglasses and Vietnamese hat sipping Hanoi beer. Stayed the night on Cat Ba Island and then did the return trip in the morning. So peaceful and relaxing.

I must say I have found Hanoi a shock to my system, especially the heat and humidity, and I know I have become dependent on our little group. I suppose it's natural when we have done everything together – eating, sightseeing, and just learning not to get killed on these crazy streets.

I have enjoyed the food and so far we have avoided dog, cat and monkey. Restaurants advertising Thit Cho, which is dog meat, are very numerous, but at least there are signs, which helps to keep the animal lovers away. Snake wine is horrific; big jars are everywhere with dead snakes coiled up in the liquid.

Tomorrow I leave at twelve to view my new home in Tien Yen and meet some of the people who I shall be working with. It takes about seven hours by car to make that journey of two hundred and sixty kilometres.

I'll write again soon,
Love Mum

Tien Yen, Vietnam
30 August 2001

After euphoria at the sight of the green rice fields and magical mountains, lotus and buffalo, peaceful scenes in contrast to the hubbub of Hanoi, I am downcast for the first time. It has been almost two weeks since I arrived and my tired eyes have had to absorb everything. I have been a sponge and just soaked it all up, and when it has been too much I have sent epistles home, and when I wrote I was able to collect my thoughts just for those few moments. In Hanoi I used the hotel as a refuge. I could turn on the air conditioning, have a shower and lie on clean sheets.

Tonight I am fighting the tears. I had my first meal made by Hang (the cook) and it was so good – prawns, fish, vegetables and the inevitable Hanoi beer. Then I unpacked my meagre possessions onto the spare bed; they looked so pitiful and so familiar and I was so homesick. All I have is a bed and a mosquito net and a bare bulb. No carpet, furniture or curtains, and the door to the balcony doesn't even fit properly. Xuan, my colleague and fellow project worker, assures me that there are no snakes, and that if there were any she would eat them… *ngon* (delicious)!

We had only met briefly at the SCF office in Hanoi, but I was struck by Xuan's lively personality and her happiness to see me. I was so glad that she was going to be with me here in Tien Yen. With her shoulder-length hair tied back in a pony tail, and wearing lime green pyjamas, she sat at the table after dinner and tried to give me an idea of what Tien Yen was like.

Tien Yen nestles along a wide, lazy river that meanders to the sea, and when you stand and look from the bridge that separates the two parts of the town, your eyes are drawn up to the misty mountains that run for two hours to the border with China. The only traffic is the passing trucks and buses that stop occasionally en route from the south. The town itself is small and remote but it has two main streets, two markets, a large primary and secondary school, a hospital and a good selection of shops and restaurants. The architecture is quite pretty, even though it is run down, and the local landscape is very beautiful. The main population of the surrounding communes is of the Dao and San Chi ethnic groups, and I would see some of these people occasionally in the town when they came into the market. Xuan assured me that they still wear their traditional costumes, and that I would easily recognise the Dao women by their shaven heads and tall red box hats, and the San Chi women by their hair severely pulled from a middle parting into a bright green scarf that is reminiscent of a child's headband. I was looking forward to exploring.

Xuan told me that everyone would be very interested in what I wore, what I did, what I ate, what I bought when I went shopping, and how much everything cost me. She warned me that I would probably gather a crowd every time I went out, at first anyway.

Keeping all this in mind, I went for a walk. It was very dark and the streets were mainly lit by the shop lights as there were no streetlights; compared to Hanoi, there was a feeling of domesticity and family life. People were less frenetic somehow, and all were very curious about me. Many said 'hello' or '*Xin Chao*'. Children were inquisitive; '*Chi ay la giao vien*,' they were told; no matter what country it is, children want to see what the teacher looks like.

I am the only Westerner here, so I shall have to make an effort with my language learning. There is just so much to think about, but it's just as well as it's the only way to stop longing for home and the people that I miss.

I think I feel down tonight because this is it. Now there's

no hotel to escape to, and this simple, poor way of life is to be mine for two years...

I wrote that last night, and when I woke up I had an adventure with a spider. Woke so early with the public loud speaker system, which stands like an Eiffel Tower in each town, blasting out some military march tunes and then a 'Good Morning Vietnam' programme with special 'thoughts for today'. I made my way down the stairs, through the cavernous house with only a small kitchen table and four chairs as decoration, and found the loo (all in the dark). I switched on the light and when I put my hand up to get some paper... Oh my God... there was a spider as big as the palm of my hand, and I couldn't run anywhere! Talk about taking deep breaths. I sprinted back to bed and huddled beneath the net, wondering what horrors were beneath it.

After breakfast my zip broke, so Xuan took me to the local dressmaker, who whipped off my trousers and gave me some elegant granny pyjamas to wear whilst she did the repair job. Meanwhile about ten women all gathered round enquiring about all my inner secrets! We all smiled at each other as they discussed my waistline, how many children I had had, how I compared with them and how much I had paid for my earrings. They laughed a lot, so I hoped that Xuan's translation was accurate.

We met the Director of Education in Tien Yen today, Mr Thuy, and drank tea from tiny cups that were constantly refilled; it was all very formal. After the meeting in the school office, he took us to his parents' house nearby. We had more tea, sitting in a small room with very large lacquer furniture, and the old couple made us very welcome. I had to smile as I made my way out of their stately living room, as the whole area in front of the house was covered with corn on the cob drying in the sun.

After the social calls, Xuan and I drove off into the

mountains with the SCF driver, Mr Trinh, to visit one of the more remote schools. I have only been that scared once before, on a roller coaster in Aberdeen, for there was no real road, and eventually we had to abandon the Landcruiser and walk the last hour to the school. The countryside was like Shangri La, just so beautiful. Rolling rice fields swirled in contours round the hillsides, dark green and mauve mountains in the distance. We walked through small hamlets of cement or wooden shacks with dark and dusty interiors, with only open fires on the cement floors for cooking, constantly boiling water or rice. The unventilated rooms were smoky, and pot-bellied children and smiling women stood in the doorways as smoke tendrils curled around them, pleased to see the visitors pass by.

The school year has not resumed yet, so the building was quiet and empty, but we did drink tea with the teachers who live there. I had great reservations about the cups, which were dirty, chipped and had tide marks from previous users, so I just watched to see if Xuan actually drank.

I wandered outside and came to a building that was little more than a hovel; there was a pig with twelve piglets and some children were playing. They were partially naked and when I came up closer I could see they were playing with some grasshoppers. They had tied the insects' legs together with thread so that they couldn't hop off. Actually it looked quite fun, though only a few short weeks ago I was lecturing the children in Stockbridge to be kind to God's creatures.

After we drove back, I looked at the makeshift map of where we had actually been, where the main road stopped and the rough red track began. I thought of the people who live there walking all that way to get to market, or to catch a bus to Tien Yen. It was certainly a revelation to me, and I wondered how many more towns and schools were hidden away in the mountains.

I've been in Tien Yen for these two days to see where I shall be living, meet my colleagues and visit schools. It is supposed to give me an idea of life in a small town in rural Vietnam and a chance to buy anything essential when I go back to Hanoi. I think a torch might be an idea!

Hanoi, 7 September 2001

My dear Gerry,

You keep asking about the Metropole. Clare and I finally broke away from the VSO lads and went to see this queen of hotels. It is a turn of the century landmark, renovated by the Sofitel chain, and just sprawls in colonial splendour east of Hoan Kiem Lake in the centre of Hanoi. We cruised into the bar, ordered gin and tonics, and sat like ladies. We were going to say that we were Russian hookers or air hostesses if anyone talked to us, thinking it would sound more exotic and exciting than volunteers, but no one did, so we just staggered back to our more humble hotel full of gin.

Outside there was a huge crowd, and at the centre we were appalled to find an old man wrapped up in Gladwrap or cellophane. He was propped up in a cyclo, with a jar of incense sticks wedged between his thigh and the side of the seat. He had just died on the pavement and this was how he was to be transported to the morgue. I often look at cyclos now, idly wondering if the passengers are for this world or the next.

That reminds me of the journey back to Hanoi from Tien Yen, when we passed a road accident. The vehicle was still immersed in the rice paddy, black smoke coming out of the bonnet. The bus that it had hit was on the verge and all the people were milling about. None of this is unusual, in any country, but beside the road was a very ornate red and gold coffin, all ready to receive the remains. No ambulance was needed, obviously, but it all looked so immediate. I wondered if someone in the next village had donated the coffin, or maybe the bus carried one (just in case).

I wondered if the body was to be taken and washed and prepared for burial. Did this one not get wrapped in Gladwrap? Was there no need to keep it clean, maybe for police evidence? So many questions, and I just had Mr Trinh, who doesn't speak English, and I can only ask 'How much?' in Vietnamese. It is so frustrating.

With a population of eighty million people, mostly compressed into high-density cities and towns, it is hard to enforce driving tests and speed restrictions, so road deaths take huge numbers each year. I'm sure not everyone has a coffin waiting for them at the side of the road though.

There were big rains on our way back down; the poor buffalo were confused since the rivers were at the same level as the roads. We stopped to eat at a restaurant near Halong Bay and there was a cage with two baby bears in it. They were so sweet, it's the first time I have ever seen a baby bear. I wonder what will happen to them when they grow up...

I am constantly mesmerised by the sights that unfold in front of my eyes on every street. Cyclos, bicycles and motorbikes transporting live, squealing pigs squashed into rattan baskets; dead pigs stretched backwards with their sliced bellies open to the world; beautiful small brown cows trussed up with no dignity on the back of a scooter, the head lolling just inches from the road; great sheets of glass being held horizontally; massive black lacquered wardrobes strapped with old bits of string onto the back of a bike; tall palm trees perched behind the driver and rising high above the traffic. Once I saw a naked mannequin sitting between the driver's arms; that did make me do a double take. I have seen a huge teardrop chandelier clink past, and a bright blue Bambi from a fairground carousel. Different equations of families are transported, sometimes all four on a bike.

Once, years ago, driving along the shore of Loch Ness we came across a police 'incident'. A van transporting a huge model of the Loch Ness Monster (en route for the tourist centre in Drumnadrochit) had been involved in a minor accident. One of Nessie's flippers had been protruding too far out, and when a car overtook, it had its paint scraped by the 'monster'. We saw the police with their notebooks and, watching all the earnest questioning, I thought of the future insurance claim, and wondered how it would read.

I can't believe Natasha is nineteen already. I did hear from her, and she and Nick and Marie seem to be getting on all right in

Australia. It's strange when you have children and suddenly they are so grown up that they are living on the other side of the world and leading independent lives. It happens so slowly that you don't really notice the change.

I had to laugh at your big resolves to find a 'hobby'... I shall wait and see what you come up with. Poor Jinx sounds as though he needs special cat counselling, with all his family leaving so quickly. Maybe his new adopted one is more stable.

When I was in Tien Yen I decided to start my new diary and have began to record all my experiences. I hadn't expected to feel so lonely or isolated. When I write down all my thoughts and impressions I feel as though I am sharing them with you.

Till the next time,

Love Mum

Hanoi, 12 September 2001

Dear Gerry,

I have not felt this unhappy for so long. Last night Clare and I came back from drinking margaritas in the Press Club to be met by Chad and Emma, who told us about the World Trade Center disaster in New York. We listened to all the news on my radio, and the thought of the awful repercussions that are bound to happen made us all feel very mortal. I tried to email, but Hotmail was impossible owing to the American crisis; there are times when everyone just wants to be with his or her own special people.

Love Mum

Tien Yen

20 September 2001

From a week of the 'glooms' when I just couldn't see my path at all, suddenly I feel on course again, and everything has regained its magic. I keep feeling I have to write everything down and I do, with the passion of a newcomer, terrified that I might forget it all.

These last few days I have been sitting in on the teacher training of the ethnic minority teachers. Experience is varied, from a little to zero. These five days will be it. What requires four years of a B Ed degree takes five days here. Of course this doesn't apply to the whole of Vietnam; its education generally boasts a high standard, but for the remote mountain areas, with little need for formal education and the collapse of the communist support money, there's scant finance for schooling. In any case, poverty is rife and it's sometimes a miracle if the children turn up at all.

We all watch four trainers from MOET (no, not champagne, but the Ministry of Education and Training in Hanoi) do their stuff. On Monday I sat feeling lost and bewildered and totally useless, with a very occasional word striking a chord from my Vietnamese lessons. I stared out of the window and saw my washing on the balcony across the street; it's crazy how the sight of something so familiar can make you so sad.

By Tuesday, however, I was entranced with the head trainer, Mr Hoan. He totally captivated me and everyone else in the room, because he has that wonderful gift of making every student feel special, and is able to inspire confidence in even the most shy of participants. I watched in awe as he clapped and sang and had everyone taking part in a group activity.

During training, Bich, my SCF boss, took me to visit one of the schools. She told me that she wants me to take charge of one of the classes and convert it into a model preschool class. I just had to photograph the room; it looks like someone's store cupboard, filthy and with one barred window. She has high hopes that I shall help to rewrite some of the curriculum and pilot modern preschool methods. I just smiled and said, 'Of course,' and thought, Bloody hell! I took lots of photos of the school and the children; maybe one day we'll compare the differences.

Mr Hoan and the other trainers got stuck into my duty-free vodka last night and sang loudly, wonderfully and very competitively at the karaoke across the road. Tonight he couldn't wait until we had finished eating, and just launched into 'Santa Lucia' so enthusiastically that he soon had us all blasting out the song. There was certainly no need for microphones.

Later, looking for a little peace and quiet, Xuan and I walked down to the river, sat on the causeway that links the two parts of Tien Yen, and stared up at the stars and the new harvest moon. This is a very special festival time in Vietnam, it marks the middle of autumn, and there are lanterns and parades and special moon cakes to eat. While we sat beside the black river and watched the lights of the town, we planned all our social activities and discussed life in Tien Yen and the problems of the 'youth of today'. If you closed your eyes you could be anywhere – drugs, unemployment, the sex industry. I was shocked, for here in this quiet town I thought it would be only tranquil buffaloes and crazy cyclists.

This afternoon I was informed that there is to be a special function tomorrow night and we will all have to perform something, so I have decided to teach my fellow trainers the eightsome reel, and I am very glad that I brought a CD of Scottish dance music. The rehearsal went well… everyone was just so enthusiastic and didn't want to get out of the middle of the circle; it truly was an awesome sight as they all whirled around to the beat of Jimmy Shand and his band! They say that wherever Scots go in the world, Caledonian Societies spring up, and the shy musician from Auchtermuchty is heard throughout all the far-flung posts that Scots find themselves in. Quite an amazing legacy.

All the young teachers are fascinated by pictures of Scotland. I showed them photos of my three children, Gerry, Nick and Natasha, and one of them asked where my husband was. '*Nhung toi da ly di* – I am divorced,' I said. Well, she just started to cry and cry. I was horrified, and I was sort of hoping that she would introduce me to a wealthy uncle with a few million buffalo. Divorce is becoming more available and acceptable in Vietnam, but in this remote area it is fairly uncommon and the family is of prime importance.

In some ways I am glad to be away from Hanoi, and start what I came out to do. When I go to the Education Forum in October I might be glad to hear the city beeps again, though, for apart from the odd rumble of buses and trucks on their way to China it is fairly quiet. The area I'm in, Quang Ninh Province, is the main coal mining area of Vietnam, and its northern area borders with China. The large border crossing of Mong Cai sees a high level of trade, where Chinese merchants and tourists come over to Vietnam for the day and Vietnamese traders go over to the Chinese side. Many of the shopkeepers in Tien Yen stock their businesses in this way. The rest of the people in the area are mainly engaged in farming, and the further up in the mountains you go, the poorer are the people living there, and access to schools and healthcare becomes more of a problem. I've yet to see just how much of a problem the schooling is. The daunting thing is that I'm expected to be part of the solution.

I am being dosed up with quite a few of the local remedies; all the local ladies are concerned at my persistent cough, and all have their own ideas for home elixirs. I was sent to bed last night with an amazing nightcap, *che do den*, made from black beans that have been boiled in a sugar mixture. It tastes quite nice. You drink the liquid then spoon up the beans and eat them. It is supposed to be very cooling.

Xuan took me to meet Mrs Mai, a neighbour who runs a large guesthouse up the street. She and her husband and grown-up son have been a wonderful support for all the staff of SCF over the years, and even now they are able to house all the teachers when they come into town from the outlying areas for training sessions. She is motherly and kind, and I was given a big warm welcoming hug. Xuan and I were given tea in tiny cups – quite minty and *ngon lam* (very delicious). I asked if it was green, but no, she showed me the packet and I read on the side 'very good for hepatitis' and 'sound sleep'.

I am lucky to be living on a river and being able to eat from a market overflowing with fish, crabs, prawns and mountains of greenery. Crazy fruits like dragon fruit and custard apples, as well as all the usual papayas, mangoes and limes find their way to our table, so why have I had a cough ever since I came to Vietnam? Even after consuming two bottles of potion that came in a box with a very graphic picture of red lungs complete with blue and red veins threaded through them, I was given yet another concoction. It was made from lotus seeds, painstakingly prepared then boiled and thickened with cornflour, but it seems it is just another remedy for sleepless nights. I actually do not have a problem in that department.

I thought I might, though, after seeing a whole barbecued dog in the market place. I had been warned, but it was still terrible... the teeth were clenched tight in the blackened face. Baby bears in cages; whole creatures brought to the table on plates, including their tails; and the few cats that I have seen wearing collars and tied up. You could deduce that the Vietnamese have little sentiment about pets or animals or preserving the environment. Of course there are always exceptions, and there are animals that are loved and cosseted, and I believe there are some very committed environmentalists, but at this stage I am just aware of my radical introduction to a culture that I do not understand.

My short-wave radio has kept me in touch with all the tragic events in America and I remember sitting with the other volunteers in Hanoi, huddled around it stunned with disbelief. When we talked to the local hotel staff, I think they gave us a considered, diplomatic response, but when discussing the events with my Vietnamese friend's husband, he smiled and said, 'Do you want my real response?' Of course this was coloured by his memory of his home and street being bombed in the 'American War', and the days he spent pulling friends and family from the rubble and effectively losing everything.

I am weary, no further adventures with spiders or snakes… yet!

Tien Yen, 28 September 2001

My dearest Gerry,

It was so good hearing your voice; I was on a high for ages. Then Nick called from Australia, full of his news and plans, so I feel very loved and wanted at the moment... hope it lasts!

I have been relaxing this morning, sitting on my balcony listening to the badminton fanatics next door. I then did my washing by hand, squatting down with a large plastic bowl, Omo and the cold tap... felt very virtuous, and didn't miss the Zanussi at all. I then started on my tapestry that I have been trying to finish for the last four years, had lunch and then an afternoon sleep. I should probably go for a gentle stroll later, and then I will have completed a very sedate Jane Austen sort of day.

On our visit to schools yesterday Mr Trinh bought a chicken from a San Chi lady nestling under a purple umbrella. It squawked all the way back in the Landcruiser and kept escaping and getting under my feet. I felt very disconcerted as it stared at me knowingly with its beady eye. Anyway Hang killed it, boiled it, and it was on the table for lunch. I could barely swallow it as boiled chickens can be quite tough unless you get the breast. I keep fantasising about ovens and the glorious smell of roasting meat, but I can't really complain as Hang manages miracles on her two gas burners.

I was deeply grieved on Monday seeing a lovely dog being squashed into a basket on the back of a bike. It was yelping with fear and looking at its traitor of a master with such trust. It was off to market, and I was just about crying. I also saw a basket full of kittens and puppies in the market. I do so want a cat, but am scared it would get stolen.

This last week we have visited a lot of schools. The SCF jeep has hurled us around and I've had every cliché in the book: white knuckles, stomach knots, everything. Yesterday was the worst; I really feel the Vietnamese lessons should have included phrases like,

'Get help; we're all going to die.'

The school we travelled to on Monday was way out in the wilderness and we had to walk the last mile and a half and cross a large river. Xuan fell in, soaking my camera, as she had been taking a picture of me with a buffalo. She didn't look very dignified turning up at the school, soaked from the neck down; I just thanked God it wasn't me.

The highlight of this trip was meeting Mrs Thuy. I interviewed her about becoming the preschool teacher, with Xuan translating, and we could hardly get her to stop for breath as she related her life story. She met her husband after arriving in Tien Yen to look for work, and we heard of what it was like to be Kinh (the largest group in Vietnam), married to a Dau man, and living in a San Chi village. Her children speak all three languages, and Mrs Thuy herself is just perfect for teaching Vietnamese to this group of children. She told us that she had paid VND 250,000 to the government in order to have another child after her allotted two, and a further VND 250,000 when the hoped-for son and heir did not appear. Alas she now has four daughters and no one to inherit the rice fields and forest of cinnamon trees.

As she talked I had a chance to study her features, very fine though roughened, no doubt from a lack of Oil of Olay. Her hands and arms were almost those of a man's, with big sinews and muscles. She was bargaining with Xuan, saying that she would do the job, but during the rice and cinnamon harvest she would not be able to come to school.

We met her later on our way back from the remotest school, carrying a tree on her back, and she invited us into her house. It was built of homemade bricks and set high above the road, through a planted vegetable garden and beside the hillside covered in mature cinnamon trees. We sat out in the front with her very handsome husband and her father-in-law, drinking tea in very suspect cracked china while all around us chickens, dogs and children milled about. Pigs grunted in their pens and the buffalo grazed on the grass verge by the road. The view was breathtaking. I just looked at the *panorama of rice fields and the dark shadows of the teak forests and huge rolling mountains in the distance, and I listened to Mrs Thuy, watching her face, so full of pride and enthusiasm for her home and way of life.*

That's all my news for the moment; I am going to Hanoi for a week tomorrow for the Education Forum on Early Childhood Education. It should be interesting to hear how other groups operate. Whilst in town, I have big plans to start a patchwork quilt at last.

Love Mum

Hanoi

2 October 2001

I don't feel so good tonight, sitting here in the Emotion Café, probably because I had my third hepatitis B injection and it is just making me feel out of sorts. Feel like going back to the hotel and curling up and watching TV, but the news of chemical warfare and anthrax spores is not really good viewing.

Last night I went up to the lake and was mesmerised by the grannies' aerobics class. There was the tape recorder, the traffic, the tourists and these seriously old ladies charging about. I had to sit down and watch, and was amazed when they did the Dance of the Red Fan. They all did it practically in slow motion, and cracked open their fans with a flourish, whilst balancing on one leg. I was impressed.

I have become hooked on motorbike taxis, or *xe oms*. I have borrowed a helmet from SCF, so travel to work in the rush hour with my eyes tightly shut. When I arrived at the VSO office today, I was lucky that I had my hair squasher on as Agneta, our beautiful, serene Swedish programme officer, turned up just at the same time. I could be repatriated for the crime of being on a bike without a helmet.

Xuan has made me my hexagon shape, so now I have my template and I am ready to start making the quilt at last. I am going shopping with Emilda, another volunteer who lives and works in Hanoi, and we are going to buy three shades of green silk. She will help me to cut it and show me how to tack everything onto newspaper shapes, and that makes it more manageable when I come to sew it all together.

Hanoi, 6 October 2001

My dear Gerry,

I can't help noticing, as I march about the city, that people seem to spend so much time out of doors, huddled together on the pavements, eating, smoking or just drinking tea. Grannies sit on tiny stools, sporting a wonderful array of headgear, their faces etched with the wrinkles of a lifetime, and they gaze about and gossip to neighbours or bargain for fruit from passing street sellers. I am sure this must eliminate the feelings of loneliness and despair that occur in the West as a result of the scattering of family units. Social Services in Edinburgh used to be full of reports of the sadness of elderly widows and widowers who become prisoners trapped behind triple-locked doors.

Emilda and I sat down at a pavement restaurant or com bui, *which translates as a 'dust meal'. She introduced me to* pho ga. *This is simply chicken and noodles, or made with beef if you order* pho bo. *It is the dish of Hanoi, and Vietnamese all over the world search for it when they are homesick; there are also restaurants down south in Ho Chi Minh City that specialise in it. People tend to eat it for breakfast, but in Hanoi it's available at any time of the day or night, as a meal or a snack, depending how hungry you are. Sometimes you see street vendors carrying everything they need to prepare it balanced on trays at the end of their shoulder poles, complete with the little container of burning coals to heat it all up.*

We watched the pho *(pronounced 'fur') being prepared. Thin strips of rice noodles were put in a bowl, bits of boiled chicken and slices of spring onion, complete with the green stalks, were added, and then boiling hot stock flavoured with ginger and fish sauce was ladled on. We were presented with our bowl and added lemon juice, vinegar, pepper and chilli. It was so tasty, and for the exorbitant sum of only 25p.*

In the olden days, eating at home with the family was a

significant part of the day, rather like our dinnertime, but throughout two long wars the entire population became displaced. People had to work all hours, so it became necessary for food to be brought to the workplace in containers. This habit of eating together has continued, and it is seen as a sign of equality for people of all walks of life to sit and share a meal together (in the dust!). So different to our lifestyle at home, and so very companionable.

Back to Tien Yen in a couple of days, will write again soon,

Loads of love, Mum

Tien Yen
9 October 2001

I think I have asphyxiated myself by spraying mosquito spray everywhere, but I just cannot stand my feet getting bitten. The fumes are lethal and I can feel them in my throat. I survived the drive back up to Tien Yen on my own with Mr Trinh. Xuan is staying in Hanoi for another week. The stop for lunch was an experience, as we sat in silence. I tried some basic conversation, but it is painful. I mean, there is only so much you can say about farm animals, and that seems to be all that I am good at!

In the week ahead I must learn some more Vietnamese, and do some lesson preparation and paint some visual aids. And sewing! I can hardly wait to begin.

Tien Yen, 11 October 2001

My dear Gerry,

I just give up. Although I struggled hard with French, I never felt so inadequate. In Hanoi I watched Arijan, who speaks English, Dutch, French and German, make himself understood in this language where the six tones entirely change the meaning of one simple sound. For example, 'ma' can mean ghost, mother, which, tomb, horse or rice seedling, depending on which accents are used. For goodness sake! All I seem to be able to say is 'khong' which means no!

I suppose it would be worse if all the street signs were in some indecipherable script like Thai or Tamil. Post offices in every town usually have a large sign that reads 'Buu Dien', so if you have learnt basic vocabulary for words like hotel or hospital, you can actually read the signs phonetically. A special thank you for this must go to a French Jesuit missionary, Alexander de Rhodes (1591–1660), who devised the 'quoc ngu' or Latin-based phonetic alphabet. He replaced the Chinese characters with quoc ngu to make it easier for the communication of the gospel to the masses, who had not been educated to the high standards of the Mandarins.

As you may have gathered by now, Vietnamese is a monosyllabic language, so if each sound has a phonetic name symbol then it can be easily interpreted. Vietnam is really Viet Nam; similarly it is Ha Noi, Sai Gon, and Tien Yen.

I have watched Xuan write on the computer keyboard and wondered at the speed of her fingers; I am so full of admiration at her dexterity and use of language. Six different accents, like the acute, grave and circumflex used in French, are put in use and she chooses certain keys for the appropriate accented vowels. She can then switch from Vietnamese and translate into English using the English keyboard setting, and continue with her work.

By contrast I struggle on with my childish attempts at 'toi khong hieu' *or 'I don't understand', but will finish here with a flourish and a fluent 'goodnight!'*

Chuc ngu ngon, *Mum*

Tien Yen

12 October 2001

Well, what a start to the day. After being woken as usual by the rousing music and the morning headlines at the crack of dawn, I set off to the loo and have never seen anything so amazing in my whole life. The entire kitchen area was full of bats. There were so many the air was black; I am sure there were at least five hundred. I just stood there (feeling very like David Attenborough) and kept thinking, Well, they are supposed to have radar, but if they do bite, do they have rabies? I had seen the odd one in there before, and had heard them chittering in the roof space, but it was as though there was a huge black curtain being wafted in the kitchen; the room was alive with the noise of their wings. In sheer terror I screamed for Hang. She casually walked through the mass of frantic creatures and turned on the fan to its highest setting. Then she looked back at me and shook her head as though I was mad.

I had thought that my existence was back on an even keel, with no major complications like spiders or snakes. Life has taken on a gentle routine this week and it is all very silent. Xuan is still in Hanoi, so it is just Hang and I in the house. We have the Vietnamese-English dictionary to help us through the major issues.

Hang cooks for us both, and I eat and eat. I have big resolutions each day not to eat too much, but then she makes cabbage that is dipped into soft boiled egg and fish sauce, and crab omelette, and beef stir-fried with loads of vegetables, and water melon, and I have to reassure myself that it is all good stuff; no sweeties or chocolates. I have visions of the new improved lean, mean fighting machine that will waltz out of here one day.

I have been watching Hang cook, and although there are only two of us, she goes to the same amount of trouble as if she was cooking for ten. I accompanied her to the market this morning and we squatted companionably as she haggled over spring onions and pieces of tofu. '*Dat Qua* – too expensive!' she cried, as she beat the price down to VND 1,000; about 5p. We moved from stall to stall and the basket filled with tomatoes, squid, pork and a whole collection of leaves. The only ones I recognised were the feathery fronds of dill and the pungent Vietnamese mint; the rest looked like a variation of the garden nettle. I remember vowing in Hanoi that I would never shop for food in the local market. Now here I was, only a few weeks later, discussing and handling pieces of pork and watching it get minced through a very elaborate machine that would probably be a museum piece in Scotland.

Later I watched Hang put the pork mince, fish sauce, eggs, shredded dried mushroom, spring onions, oil and black pepper into a bowl and mix it together until it looked like a hamburger or meat loaf mix. She then flattened the mixture like a pancake and fried it till it was brown on both sides. This was 'omelette', and we ate it with the leaves, dipped in fish sauce, sugar, chilli and garlic. So simple yet so delicious.

I have been painting pictures as visual aids for schools, and yesterday I did a huge picture with loads of creatures and all the Vietnamese words pinned on. I could barely straighten up at the end of the day, as I had been bent over for hours on the floor. I had to laugh out loud the day before yesterday, as I had drawn all the pictures of *A Very Hungry Caterpillar*: 'on Monday he ate one apple'... remember the story? Whilst I was in the process of stapling the pictures to the word pages to create a makeshift book, Hang came along to see what I was up to. She decided to help. She is quite a character and makes a funny clicking

45

sound as she shakes her head, a bit like a bushman from the Kalahari. She does this continually when she has any contact with me. As she corrected my words and took over the stapling job, she got the Vietnamese-English dictionary and pointed to '*su ba hoa mat thi gio*', which translates as 'what a palavar'. She was right, of course!

I read a lot, prepare lessons, and have started to sew my patchwork quilt. I have now completed four hexagonal flowers… it is going to take an age. I feel so like a medieval queen in a castle, stitching away, or the Lady of Shalot, thinking my thoughts and trying to learn the words for Santa Lucia in Vietnamese. Maybe I should make a quilt for each of my children: green for Vietnam (Natasha), white for Mongolia (Gerry), and probably tartan for Scotland (Nick). Well, that's my life's plan made.

Hang and I are going cycling to the beach at Mua Chua on Sunday, on some rickety old bikes. It is about ten miles to the sea, and we shall take a little picnic of bread, squashed pork, cucumber and some water… not your typical Scottish picnic. I feel all this reading and sewing needs to be offset with some activity.

Next week this little idyll will be over when Mr Trinh and Xuan get back and we are off doing great things at the preschool at Dong Moc, so I am enjoying the peace and tranquillity whilst I have it. I am reading *The God of Small Things*. Oh Lord the pain; it is so poignant and evokes such strong memories of childhood, but thank goodness not for me the mind-numbing sadness of the denouement!

I feel suspended in time, in a retreat, a private and self-imposed prison. After all, the front door is open, and I am doing all my hobbies. Perhaps I am just shunning going outside as for a while I want to remain invisible and be away from the voluble curiosity that meets me wherever I go. It is the old pleasure of seeing the rain on the windowpane, enjoying the melancholy, and having a good excuse not to have to do the gardening or cut the grass. It won't last, but it is a wonderful indulgence after eight weeks of being constantly with people.

Yesterday was my birthday, and for the first time ever there were no cards. Memories of other years flooded in, of flowers, chocolates, champagne and funny homemade cards from the children at all ages, and so this one seemed odd and a little sad. The day began with a crack-of-dawn start to visit the opening of a new preschool class in Ba Che. We stopped and collected the local VIPs from the Education Office, including the Chairman of the People's Committee, two headmasters and two important ladies. They all crammed in the back, and the dyed blonde with the Gucci sunglasses (me) sat up in the front looking like Princess Anne's representative for Save the Children. Oh dear, what a farce. Don't they know that I am just a riff-raff, hoi-polloi VSO?

We survived the journey, passing some amazing Dau ethnic minority ladies in fantastic outfits: black tunics over knee-length trousers, the edges all embroidered red and white, and of course, as is also traditional, on their bald, shaved heads were the tall red hats. Because it was hot and sunny, they had placed the Vietnamese conical hat on top! It looked a bit like a child's building set of geometric shapes. They dress like this every day, just to tend the buffalo and brush out the front room.

After the ceremony at the school, where all the important VIPs made speeches to the collected audience of Xuan, about sixteen five-year-olds and me, we gave the children some sweets and then were treated to a banquet of fruit. The whole mood was so friendly and generous, and good wishes and hugs were exchanged. I couldn't believe so much effort had gone into this opening ceremony, but it proves the People's Committee and the Education Office are committed to improving education in this district, which is one of the poorest in the region. Morale boosting is important, no matter where you are.

When I got back I decided to give myself a birthday treat: a shampoo in a local shop specialising in this! It was divine. There was a see-through net curtain dividing the area between the hair salon and a ping-pong joint next door. All the lads were shouting '*Mot! Hai!*' whilst I lay on the 'dentist's chair' with my head in a red baking bowl and was rubbed and massaged and pummelled and had a full facial as well. That was a surprise; suddenly I felt the warm water trickle over my forehead and then she started on my cheeks and face. The whole thing lasted for forty-five minutes and cost VND 5,000; about 25p.

I cruised back to the house (with mascara ingrained under my eyes, I looked like a relaxed corpse) and found Xuan and Mr Trinh cooking the meal of the century. When I had sorted out my face, I went downstairs to a banquet with candles, rice wine and beer. I was presented with a huge bunch of flowers and a beautiful green glass horse. I couldn't believe it and just felt so overwhelmed.

Later, after eating until we nearly burst, we sang 'Santa Lucia' loudly and then chatted by candlelight. Xuan looked beautiful; her eyes go liquid when she is happy and she has the most infectious laugh and a sharp sense of humour. I have grown so fond of her in such a short time, and although she is only twenty-eight we get on so well, and she laughs at me all the time. 'Oh Gael, be patient!' she implores me whenever I want to change the world in a day. I believe it is her warmth and tactile personality that has created the trust and confidence between the chiefs, teachers and children, and it is her diplomacy that enables the project to be accepted and ideas implemented. I am growing fond of Mr Trinh as well; he is so reassuring and kind, and he makes us all feel safe and looked after. I looked at them both by candlelight and felt so lucky and happy.

Today we went to Dong Hong School to visit the teacher Mui, and while we were busy with the children, Mr Trinh bought a puppy. He is so gorgeous, black and fat with two brown paws. We are going to call him Mr Darcy as he has the look of a handsome beast. Mr Trinh calls him Darcy Dog. Already he is getting used to his new home, and when he is tired he flops with his legs straight out at the back, like a plump beanbag with paws.

Tien Yen
25 October 2001

I hold my head in shame. I came here full of noble ideas of creating the perfect setting for small children to learn a second language. I had the vision in my head of recreating an Edinburgh situation in rural Vietnam. Even after many visits to the schools in Tien Yen District, I was still optimistic and continued to paint murals for the classrooms with the vocabulary that children use daily and can relate to.

Until today. We drove up into the mountains to Binh Lieu district and took a left across a river where the water flowed fast and went right over our wheels (my little Honda would have drowned). Diggers and lorries were constructing a road and the whole place was swarming with military. This area borders China and they have a troubled history. Even as recently as 1999 there have been skirmishes over trivialities, so there is still a feeling of sensitivity and high security. Dau ladies walked about in their wonderful costumes, and children with little or nothing on jumped in and out of the bushes. The whole atmosphere was surreal.

Eventually we visited the school. Children swarmed around us, many with injuries – a lost eye, a vicious burn down the neck and shoulders, the usual colds – but it's the rags that really mark this area from the market fashion of Tien Yen, where you see green floral shirts for boys and gaudy sugary pink for the girls. I remember thinking it was a uniform when I first saw them. These children today have little, and what they do have is ripped and definitely passed down many times.

I sat in with the preschool teacher. It is her first job since the training with us in September. It was grim. Rows of waifs sat on small red stools along the blank, stained walls, and she was standing very tall (in high heels) in front. Because of the visitors (us), the village turned out to watch. Grannies, aunties, everyone crowded the door and window to have a look. With my pathetic attempts at Vietnamese I tried to change the seating arrangements, and convinced the teacher to sit down and gather the children around her, and so be at their level. We talked about the vocabulary of the body, then gave the children a chalkboard each. Although they were five years old, none of them had ever held a writing implement before, so they weren't quite sure what to do with it. It was quite a task. Anyway, the end result was inspiring, and funny faces were drawn, shown, named and admired (by the whole village). A song was sung, encouragement given to the teacher, a bag of supplies from SCF donated, promises made for pictures to cover the filthy, empty walls, and we were off.

Mr Trinh had a bag of star aniseed that had been drying beside the road, and it now filled the car with the most pungent aroma; it was bliss after the dank school. We visited the border and looked across the river to China, saw the flag waving, and didn't take any photos after the policeman told me to put my camera away. We had lunch and I sat and watched the headmaster, the deputy, the clerk and a VIP lady guzzling the rice wine, chattering raucously, and words like 'Taliban' filtered through. In fact it infiltrates everywhere, I suppose.

I have digressed as usual, but I was rudely awoken today from my dreams of home corners and drawing tables and dressing-up clothes for imaginative play; all perfectly good ways to learn to speak and use vocabulary. I spent the morning with a piece of chalk in my hand in a filthy room with no furniture except tiny plastic chairs, no toys, no paper, no crayons, and children who looked in awe at the box of pathetically small delights that we had brought. I hope the photos come out, and hope that one day we can look and contrast the great improvements.

All that somehow goes side by side with the idyllic setting of tall pointy mountains, whispery bamboo, delicate fronds and rice fields that curve around the river and rise in tiers up the hillsides. Red earth gouged out of the hillsides fills the roadside kilns, and fresh red bricks are cooled in neat rows ready to be loaded onto MASH-style trucks. They look like toys except for the vile black smoke that belches from their exhausts. Oh to be a farmer, in a little home-made house, with banana trees and chickens and a big beautiful buffalo, and a view that would inspire poetry, songs and a hammock!

Well, nice to look at, anyway. I am off now to shower and shampoo... I just hope I don't have nits.

Balcony, Hang Gai Street, Hanoi
July 2002

I can still hear Xuan's voice saying, 'Be patient, Gael.' I wonder how many times she said that to me last year.

I would sit at the Save the Children office in Hanoi and try to absorb the key issues affecting children: poverty; child labour; disability; sexual exploitation and abuse; education; HIV/AIDS. As I read the accounts, people all around me were busy writing reports, planning field trips, writing proposals, exchanging and sharing news from each project that stretched from the Chinese border in the north right through the central regions down to Ho Chi Minh City in the south. I was impressed with all the good work and dedication that went into all these issues, though sometimes as I read a report the wording would make me chuckle. One report noted the advantages of preschool education as, 'The children are now fearless, courageous, innocent and groovy.' Another underlined the worry of HIV/AIDS in small villages where husbands have to go away to supplement family income. One wife advised her husband 'in case of "utmost joy" he cannot forbear himself, then he should use a condom. It is hard for wife to advise spouse like that.'

Before I left the UK I had a meeting with Anne Mulcahy, the head of the Asia desk for SCF in London. She briefed me on where I would be and what ethnic groups I would be involved with.

I remember reading about Vietnam as being one of the world's most densely populated countries. More than eighty-five percent of its seventy-eight million people are ethnic Vietnamese, or Kinh, who mostly live in lowland areas. Mountainous regions are populated by more than fifty minority groups whose culture and language are distinct from the Kinh and who have kinship ties to groups in China, Laos and Thailand. Most ethnic minorities live in poor, remote parts of the country.

I read about the long struggles for independence that this country has had to endure. First came the Chinese, who dominated for almost one thousand years until the year 939 AD, and saw Vietnam as an extension of their land south of the Yellow River. The words 'Viet Nam' mean 'people of the south'.

Even after independence, there followed a series of dynasties that shaped and consolidated the country that was now united under strong ruling families. Chinese culture exerted a very strong influence on the fledgling Viet Nam, as the Royal Courts and the elite retained the Chinese language and traditions, and Confucianism remained dominant in the areas of social and political morality. The use of classical Chinese as the official language in all documents was maintained, and for students and ambitious young men, the highest scholastic achievement was to become a mandarin.

A mandarin was an official in the imperial bureaucracy, with very high status. Students sat a series of gruelling examinations in order to achieve this title, for it was stipulated in the teachings of Confucius that only men of culture were qualified to protect the welfare of the people. Thus the examinations were based on Chinese literature, history and poetry. When the students graduated, these wise, virtuous, educated men became civil servants and commanded great respect and veneration from all, though in fact they had a meagre income and were only a little better off than the people that they governed. As the majority of people were illiterate, it was to the scholars and mandarins that they came when they needed anything recorded, or prayers written in order to communicate with the various deities.

The next colonisation began when the French arrived in

1859. This saw an end to the imperial way of life, and the scholars and mandarins became the puppets for the real power that came from France. The country was divided into three protectorates – Annam, Tonkin and Cochinchina – and an uneasy peace prevailed. Once the Vietnamese realised that the French intended to stay for a long period, they concentrated on improving their own situation, and many collaborated with the French.

During the Second World War the Japanese occupation force briefly replaced the French, until Japan surrendered in 1945. Ho Chi Minh, the leader of the Independent Movement, took the opportunity to declare the 'Democratic Republic of Vietnam' on 2 September 1945. France was unwilling to give up its colony without a fight, so this ultimately resulted in a ten-year war that eventually saw the French defeated in the now famous battle at Dien Bien Phu in 1954. At peace talks held in Geneva, the country was divided. The north became a Socialist country with ties to the Soviet bloc, whilst the south was capitalist and pro western. The stage was now set for what became known in the West as the Vietnam War, and in the East as 'The War of American Aggression'.

This appalling period of history was ultimately a failed attempt by South Vietnam and the US to prevent the North Vietnamese communists from uniting the country under their leadership. By 1968 it had become an increasingly American war, with more than 500,000 US troops fighting. The results and tragedy of this war can still be seen in rural life today, and in some cases the Vietnamese people are still dying and suffering terrible injuries, almost thirty years later: the evidence of the B52 bomb attacks; the constant deaths by undetected land mines; babies born deformed as a result of contamination by poisons and toxins; and the dreadful legacy of Agent Orange that had been sprayed to eradicate all life and vegetation.

By the time the Communists entered Saigon in 1975, thus ending the war, millions of lives had been lost. Almost immediately Vietnam was drawn into yet another war as a result of Cambodian attacks on Vietnamese villages. Vietnamese troops were sent into Cambodia in December 1978, toppling the Khmer Rouge regime. China, who backed the Khmer Rouge, retaliated by starting a war on Vietnam's northern border. Vietnam withdrew from Cambodia in 1989 and Sino-Vietnamese relations have greatly improved in recent years. In 1995 diplomatic relations were restored with the US, and Vietnam became a member of the Association of South East Asian Nations (ASEAN).

The Communist Party is still the central force in Vietnam. About eighty percent of deputies in the National Assembly are party members. Government policy is set by the eighteen-member Politburo, which is elected by the 170-member Central Committee at party congresses held every five years. Until his death in 1969, Ho Chi Minh dominated Vietnamese politics. Now four men hold the top leadership posts of Party General Secretary, Prime Minister, President and Chairman of the National Assembly. The People's Army of Vietnam, which saw off three of the world's most powerful armies – the French, American and Chinese – has deep roots in Vietnamese society, and military men occupy many positions of authority. Ho Chi Minh is still revered as the beloved uncle of his people. His photograph is found in every home, office and public building. His portrait adorns every schoolroom in every city and village, and the Great Man himself lies in diminutive splendour in his giant mausoleum in Hanoi. Great crocodiles of people line up patiently in the sun waiting their turn to see his embalmed body.

Vietnam remains an agricultural society, with eighty percent of the population living in rural areas and seventy percent of the labour force employed in agriculture and forestry. Everywhere you look you see the legacy of a campaign that was once called 'An Inch of Land is an Inch of Gold'. To prevent starvation, every piece of land had to be cultivated with food crops, and even today people still plant lettuces, maize and soybeans in the tiny spaces between fields or gardens.

Commercially, Vietnam is the world's second largest exporter of rice. With two monsoon seasons a year, many areas can produce two crops annually from the same land. Rubber, coffee and sugar cane are also major crops, and the country has significant reserves of oil. Mining, particularly for coal, is important in the north. Ironically, Vietnam has largely untapped sources of hydropower, yet most of the countryside lacks electricity. The main source of energy in rural homes is wood from forests, but with the effects of war damage, increasing population pressure and clearance of forests for growing crops, people find it harder and harder to gather or buy enough wood for their stoves.

The US-led aid and trade embargo after the war forced Hanoi to rely increasingly on economic and military aid from the Soviet Union. In 1986, Vietnam mirrored their protector by beginning a process of economic restructuring known as Doi Moi, similar to the perestroika occurring in the Soviet Union. The Doi Moi reforms really took hold in 1988 when the government began to distribute land from cooperative farms to individual farmers. In industry, subsidies to state enterprises were drastically reduced and measures introduced to encourage the development of a private sector.

Vietnam's economy, which had been shattered by decades of war, was again shaken in the late 1980s with the disappearance of the Soviet bloc support. Even so, ten years of market reforms had generated rapid economic growth – eight to nine percent a year in the early 1990s – and a dramatic reduction in poverty levels. In 1992 the World Bank estimated that fifty percent of the population lived below the poverty line. By 1998 this figure had decreased to thirty-five percent.

Vietnam was widely predicted to be Asia's next 'economic tiger', but by the late 1990s the impact of the financial crisis in neighbouring countries had dampened such dreams. Foreign investment fell sharply, and Vietnam lost major export markets in the region. The repercussions of the economic slowdown were felt first in cities, where export industries are concentrated. Government leaders and foreign donors are worried that the gains made in poverty alleviation in the past decade might be eroded.

Vietnam has an official adult literacy rate of ninety-four percent; an impressive achievement for a low-income country that has experienced decades of turmoil. But its health service, once a model for other developing countries, has deteriorated since subsidies were reduced with the introduction of the Doi Moi market reforms. At the same time, private health services have emerged and are competing with and complementing the state system, but of course these private services are only available to those who can afford it. New health problems are also putting pressure on the public health system. The most serious is the HIV/AIDS epidemic, which has spread rapidly as drug use and commercial sex activity have increased. Other major social problems include rising unemployment and a widening gap between rich and poor. Not dissimilar problems to those in Scotland...

From reading the Country Information facts in the office in London, I had a picture in my head of a country that was still feeling the effects of the 1980s, and I had been prepared for squalor, poverty and a very low standard of living. But the capital city, Hanoi, has changed in the ten years since many travel writers and anthropologists had filed their reports.

There was no feeling of disillusionment amongst the city dwellers of 2001. In fact there are thousands of people who own their own motorbikes and sport clean, fashionable clothes, depicting vibrancy and a growing wealth amongst the young trendsetters. Mobile phones are now as commonplace in Hanoi as they are in Helsinki.

I got my first taste of this on the flight from Bangkok, when I flicked through the glossy in-flight magazine. There was the fashion section depicting beautiful girls with long, silky, black hair and willowy bodies modelling the Vietnamese national dress. This is the ultra-sexy, 'revealingly unrevealing' *ao dai*. It is a two-piece outfit that clings to every curve; the long, coloured tunic splits on either side of the waist, usually to reveal white, slinky satin trousers. It may hug the body but almost every inch of female flesh is covered, from the mandarin neck collar to the tapered sleeves at the wrists down to the thin ankles.

There were pages of fashion outlets for tourists to buy Vietnamese silk, lacquerware and embroidered tableware, and more colourful pages showing restaurants where meals are served in beautiful surroundings. Like any modern city, the selection is as international as the growing clientele. The magazine featured well-written articles focusing on cultural events in both Ho Chi Minh City and Hanoi, as well as features on the beautiful embroidered tapestries of Da Lat and the tailoring expertise of Hoi An.

This new Vietnam was presenting itself as gentle and graceful, and I was to find on the streets of Hanoi not a legacy of war and pain, but a city full of flowers of every shade and variety. Visitors go away now with images of roses and lilies, the colours blurred as though they had all run together on an artist's palette. The street vendors call continuously for passers-by to buy their blooms. The red of roses has replaced the blood that has been such a tragic feature of this land for so long.

One of the many legacies left by the French, apart from excellent bread and coffee, are the huge trees that form avenues on the wide streets of Hanoi. Around Hoan Kiem Lake, or the Lake of the Restored Sword, there are leisurely walkways and stone benches where people play checkers under the copiously weeping willows, or just contemplate the pagoda in the middle of the watery expanse.

For me, it is the banyan tree that epitomises all the grandeur and dignity of Vietnam. Its huge, solid, gnarled girth forms through many decades of sending down new roots. Dropping down from the high canopy are great fringes of rope-like vines that form a ghostly curtain, hiding all the nooks and crannies that house tiny altars and smoking incense sticks. The fringes are often trimmed straight with no-nonsense precision, like a schoolboy's haircut. Otherwise these floating creepers would cause havoc with electricity wires. The pavements often show signs of internal eruption as the great roots dislodge the paved walkways. From my balcony on Hang Gai Street, I look out at the banyan tree across the road and wonder what stories it could tell…

For the sake of ten years, we must plant trees.
For the sake of one hundred years, we must educate the people.

Ho Chi Minh

The main goal for the SCF project I was part of was to ensure that appropriate and relevant education provision reached children marginalised by ethnicity, language and poverty. With all this in my head, I knew that my small contribution would be to coach and support the teachers, with an emphasis on activity-based teaching methods and teaching Vietnamese as a second language. The two ethnic groups that we would be involved with were the Dau, whose ladies shaved their heads and eyebrows and wore tall red boxes on their heads, and the San Chi, whose ladies coiled their hair into a green piece of cloth, then wound it round their heads leaving a magenta-pink tuft at the nape of the neck.

So much to learn, so many anthropology reports to read!

My VSO friends were all settling into their placements and, although communication was limited, some emails did get through so we could reassure each other that we were well and coping.

I found I had two new groups of friends in Hanoi. The VSO team in the office was like the mother-ship, and the SCF team became my day-to-day colleagues. Agneta, our Swedish programme officer in VSO, was like a serene anchor. No matter what I said over those ten months, she just smiled and somehow my particular bomb of the moment was defused. She befriended me, and sometimes when I was back in Hanoi we went to concerts together and just enjoyed each other's company. Bill Tod, the country director of SCF, had a similarly calming quality. He had a warm smile and easy manner which, together with far too much charm, enabled him to gain so much through his gifts of diplomacy.

Bich was our coordinator for the Education Project in Tien Yen. She spent most of the time in Hanoi, though she did make regular visits to the 'field'. I still smile as I remember when Clare rang to speak to me in Tien Yen and Bich briskly told her, 'Gael is in the field!' Images of me digging up turnips and cabbages. Bich was forty-six, recently married for the second time, and had a baby who was then about sixteen months old. She has two other grown up children and had been widowed for fourteen years. I only recently found out the name of the baby, as she was only ever referred to as 'the baby' – 'the baby is sick'; 'the baby needs the mother'. The baby is called Queen Anne, or perhaps it was Quyen Anh.

Bich's field trips consisted of herself, the baby, the baby's maid and all the paraphernalia that went with the baby. The seven-hour trip from Hanoi to Tien Yen was a nightmare as both Bich and the maid suffered terribly from carsickness. Later my translator, Thau, joined in this little band that retched miserably into plastic bags or squatted by the roadside.

Bich devised the master plans, and her two project workers, Xuan and Hiep, carried them out. Xuan had the patience of a saint and seemed to keep her face impassive as she formed the bridges between all the factions. I remember once as we were tramping back from a school that we came across a tomb surrounded by bamboo on the edge of a hillside. I commented that it was a beautiful place to spend eternity. She just shook her head and said, 'So sad to be buried here, all alone.' I miss her, and can still see her eating bowls full of rice and remaining as skinny as a piece of bamboo. I miss her enthusiasm and the potions that she brewed for us to wash our hair, her singing Santa Lucia and Autumn Leaves, her endless chatter.

Hiep was fairly new to the team. At twenty-four he was the computer whizzkid. He ran classes teaching local headmasters and their staff skills to record data and create an information network that had been sadly lacking. His easy charm, good looks and passion for the local discotheque made him a popular pin-up. He was also brilliant at ballroom dancing, and Xuan and I spent the odd lunchtime learning the cha-cha or tango.

The office in Tien Yen was a big house with three floors. From the street it looked small and only one room wide, but in fact it was about four rooms deep and the front 'room' was the parking area for the SCF's white Toyota Landcruiser. The whole household was taken care of by Hang, the cook. Hang was a pretty twenty-three-year-old who managed to market twice a day and prepare and cook two full meals for four to sixteen people. Numbers did not faze her. She cooked prawns and crabs and pork and vegetables. She killed chickens and chopped and fried. The smells would waft up to the office and then we would hear the voice, '*Xuan oi! An com!*' and down we would go to the table, where there would be spring rolls, fish and rice and mountains of green vegetables and fruit.

Upstairs was the office, which had the computers and my work table where I used to paint and prepare all my teaching aids. In the evening I used to sew and look over the top of my glasses as I talked to Xuan. Through an adjoining doorway we had access to the training room that used to echo with the sounds of forty sopranos and one loud, clear tenor. Mr Hoan would have all the women and the few men lose their inhibitions and sing until their souls rose high into the mountains.

> *Ngoai song kia co con chim non*
> *Hoa tieng hot veo von*
> *Hoa tieng hot veo von*
> *Loi hat vui say sua.*

(There is a little bird outside the window
Singing with a melodious voice
Singing with a melodious voice
Passionately deep.)

It is beautiful and the song is repeated again and again.

When I close my eyes, I can hear them and see all their faces, and see him, the great conductor, who later would sit at dinner and sing melancholy love songs or rousing opera.

My bedroom was off the office, so I had little peace or privacy and I had to walk through all the communal areas in order to get to the one bathroom located behind the kitchen on the ground floor. Xuan and the others stayed on the floor above me, and they had a small sitting room with a TV.

There were three drivers who took us from Hanoi to Tien Yen: Mr Cuong; Mr Hoi; and Mr Trinh. All were funny, kind, easy-going men. It was Mr Trinh who really looked after us. He had the qualities of the ideal husband, father, brother and friend all wrapped into one. He shelled our crabs, ordered things we liked, protected us from unwelcome advances and understood when we were frustrated, angry or just sad. His face would break into a smile, which I miss seeing, but I am glad the project team, and the teachers and children that he used to pass the time with as we visited schools, still have him. He has got to be the most skilful driver I have ever sat next to. The roads he had to negotiate were non-existent; some only consisted of boulders and dried riverbeds. He never showed signs of stress, except when he got out of the car and lit up two cigarettes at once!

Our work days were long. We visited schools, did office work and prepared materials for teacher training. In the evenings Hang would watch Korean 'noodle' films. Xuan described these long, drawn-out, complicated love stories as the 'rice and noodle triangle', whereby if the man is with his wife (rice), he wishes he was with his girlfriend (noodles), and vice versa. The dilemmas would take hours to unravel, with ponderous close-up shots over endless cups of coffee. If Hang wasn't watching movies she would wander the streets with her friends. She would dress up, paint her nails blue or green and wear high, pointy shoes.

Trinh would play cards with our neighbours, Mr and Mrs Mai, whilst Xuan and I would sit and talk about Russian films and literature. I learnt so much about her life and family and her homeland in the northwest. I would sew and she would tell me the long, involved plot of some movie that had made a great impression on her.

Later Hiep and Thau joined us. Thau became my translator; she was tiny and very beautiful. She and Hiep played a lot on the computer, and the office became so noisy with the music of Westlife, played over and over again.

Our routine did change when we got Mr Darcy. He settled well, and at first he was so small and fat that he could not get up the stairs or jump on the beds. He would play and bite and chew, then collapse in a heap and sleep. He ate rice and soup and noodles. As he grew older we tied a blue string round his neck and took him for walks to the river. The walks took forever as he stopped and sniffed and tried to capture horrid bits of rubbish to take home, where he would then hide them in the niche under the stairs. Xuan used to wash him regularly, and he always smelled of soap and shampoo. He was black and glossy and everyone knew him. 'Mr Darcy! Mr Darcy! Darcy Dog!' He was naughty, but so funny, and rapidly became a much-loved part of all our lives.

Tien Yen

30 October 2001

It's a new day and the office is looking good. We have had the carpenters fit pinboards in the training room and the office, and Xuan and I are sticking everything up. The training room really looks like an infant classroom now, with all my paintings in place. Xuan has become a cartographer and has made a good map of the three districts that we work in; Tien Yen, Binh Lieu and Ba Che. I spent the morning making a photo collage and that is quite a focal point; it shows how the project is developing and highlights personalities, schools and, of course, hundreds of children.

Yesterday was the full moon, and this is a special time for bringing fruit and flowers to the altars in each home. Nearly all the Vietnamese practise ancestor worship, and there are incense sticks and fruit offerings and pictures of deceased loved ones in the most prestigious place in every home.

Hang has had to go home to see her mother in Hong Gai City, so the lady in the house across the road has been cooking for us these last few days. She normally just runs a breakfast business, which is the traditional *pho ga*, or chicken noodle soup, served hot and spicy with lots of lime juice. She seems to enjoy her new responsibility and watches me like a hawk to see if I am enjoying everything, even though we all just stare at the Korean movie that is blasting from the TV during meals, hearing the drama being told by a Vietnamese voice that overrides the actual actor's words. I can sense that she is asking Xuan all about my personal life, so it is quite disconcerting trying to pretend that I am not aware. I have watched her enough to notice her toenails though; they are filed to sharp points and look lethal. I think she would be very scary to sleep with.

Because of the rain this week we have been housebound, so my plans for fading away to a skinny shadow have gone, as nothing seems to interfere with my appetite and the days pass with lovely meals. Today I noticed that we were eating last night's offering to the honoured ancestors from the altar on top of the wardrobe in the sitting room. They were very nice bananas.

Xuan was telling me about the whole process of death and burial; it all sounds very economical and practical. After the wonderful wake and party, the sad procession of mourners, all wearing white bandannas, proceed to place the gilded coffin into the earth. The family return after three years to exhume the bones, wash them in perfumed water and then lay them finally to rest in tombs. These are often among the rice fields that have nurtured and given life, and now give rest for the longest of sleeps. Some choose large graveyard cities, such as the massive one just out of Hong Gai City; there are so many tombs, all huddled together. I prefer the burial sites around Tien Yen... sometimes you might see a small group nestled into a hillside. Their white stones look like rows of teeth from a distance!

I thought my time was up yesterday as I got a huge electric shock when I turned off the immersion heater. The pain ran along my arm and down my leg into my foot, and I was thrown back from the wall. It was very scary, and I told Xuan that something has to be done, as that is the second time. The man that she consulted wasn't going to do anything; he just said that I must have more static in me than normal. I was really mad. Now I stand on two pairs of flip-flops and use the wooden handle of a brush to turn it off. I feel that Princess Anne would not have to suffer such indignities in her SCF work!

Tien Yen
2 November 2001

Xuan and I went by motorbike to Bin Son. I felt a bit tense as it had been raining yesterday and the road can be busy with trucks and buses. Fortunately it wasn't and it was really quite pleasant until we turned off and got on the rough stony track that leads into the hills. It was difficult to negotiate all the potholes with the two of us on the bike, so I walked quite a lot of the way. It was lovely being so close to all the plants and to hear all the noises. There is no wildlife of course, as everything gets eaten, and now I am learning not to expect anything. Just birds.

We arrived at Tam, the teacher's, house, only to find that her class had been changed to the afternoon, but she was so pleased to have visitors that we were happy to stay for tea. We were very impressed with her new house, set amongst her rice fields. It was painted pale yellow and from the outside it looked very smart. Inside, however, there was only a bed and a table, and it was very dusty. Some star fruit had been harvested and left to dry on the floor of the 'lounge'.

Outside was wonderful; a massive pink and black pot-bellied pig was having an early lunch, and all her ten babies were snout deep in some mess in the trough, just their swollen tummies and wiggly tails to be seen. They were only five weeks old. There were arrogant geese, beady-eyed ducks, scrawny chickens that looked as though they had alopecia, and a friendly yellow dog. When I took out my camera to record this rural delight, Tam rushed and got her daughters to change into pretty clothes and hair ribbons, and she put on her high heels. I duly snapped. She then got her other child, an adopted boy of five, and explained that when he was a baby his mother didn't want him and was going to throw him away, so Tam took him, and that was that; no other complications or red tape, and you could see that he has just completed this little family. He was made to put on a yellow tracksuit over his mucky shorts and he had to stand nicely and smile – it's universal this need to record our happy faces!

Later we sat on her bed and Xuan asked how much the house cost. I squirmed at the intrusiveness of asking such a personal question, but everyone is very direct and Tam was happy to tell us that it cost VND 20 million (about £1,000), and they had had to borrow half of that from relatives. The last few years, however, have been hard and very expensive. Her husband had a bad injury from a knife and was in hospital for a month, then her youngest daughter had her big toe cut off and the top of her foot hacked in a terrible accident. The men had been in the forest chopping wood and the machete came down and slashed her foot. She hopped all the way back, and Tam ran from the fields when she saw her falling over with blood pouring all over the track. They got her to the house and she lay on the floor, very faint, and had to wait for a friend to come to take her by motorbike over the hills to the hospital in Tien Yen. The fees for both hospital visits were high and the family lives close to the breadline, so it has been a tough few years.

On the way back to Tien Yen, I couldn't help comparing the fantasy that I once had of being in love, zipping down a highway on the back of a motorbike with the wind whipping through my hair, with the reality of hanging on tight to a slip of a Vietnamese girl and wearing a big rice-cooker-like contraption on my head. But I knew I wouldn't have swapped for anything, as I gazed at the kamikaze butterflies that lazily floated in front of trucks and got zapped, or just settled in a big cloud of colour on some sections of the road. Idle thoughts and so many impressions collided as the tendrils of the forest escaped on to the grass verges, and plants with huge, luxurious leaves exuded moisture that contributed to the already fecund vegetation.

As I was whisked back I reflected on the morning's visit. I may have missed visiting a class, but there will be other days. I am glad I had the opportunity to meet Tam in the familiarity of her own home, and even though it was only for a short while I was able to learn a little of what life really is like so far off the beaten track.

Tien Yen, 5 November 2001

Dear Gerry,

Please could you send me a packet of skinny pins, good quality, but they must be skinny so they don't mark the silk? The occasional pins that I see here are so fat they leave great holes, and so far I have been working with the six that Emilda gave me when I started; talk about desperate!

It has been very quiet. Xuan is away but everyone returns tomorrow and Lyn Edmonds from New Zealand is coming too. She is travelling with her sister-in-law, Diana. I just can't wait to see them.

I have now completed forty flowers; they look a bit like the flowers you see in the Far Side cartoons!

I miss wine time; I could really do with an ice cold glass of dry white wine. I used to take it all for granted; just open the fridge and slurp as I peeled the potatoes. Never mind, I shall be falling off the Buddhist wheel of curtailing all my desires tomorrow, as Lyn will be bringing some vodka, but with Mr Trinh and Mr Hoan, there might be some competition.

Love Mum

Tien Yen

8 November 2001

There are times when I feel so happy here and I just don't want to be anywhere else. I am still feeling in a rosy glow after an unexpected visit from one of my oldest friends in the world, Lyn Edmonds. She and her sister-in-law, Diana, arrived in the midst of a pile of dust from the local bus two days ago. I had been sitting on the balcony overlooking the street, and when I saw it arrive I nearly broke my neck tripping over Mr Darcy, who spends his life getting in everyone's way, and ran out and we hugged and hugged and I couldn't believe that she was actually in Tien Yen. All the local people smiled happily at this unexpected street drama.

We eventually got inside and had tea and cake and talked and gossiped and caught up with all the news of children and friends. We then inspected the premises and they did go rather quiet when they saw my room; I suddenly saw it afresh through their eyes.

I paraded them up and down the streets and took them to the river where we stood on the causeway and watched a lady squatting down washing her clothes with all the frothy detergent, then holding the garment while the clean water did a natural rinse job as it flowed through the weir. She bundled everything up, tied her basin on to the back of her pushbike and set off for home. It was very efficient and therapeutic and, as we watched, the sun set and the river grew dark and the town above us took on the look of a theatre set, a black silhouette framing the orange sky, and for a few moments all the players were off-stage and there was a feeling of quiet and peace and expectation.

We walked back, seeing the intimate scenes of daily life being enacted in houses that never seem to have their doors shut. Families were sitting together eating; televisions were on showing the same channel in each home as we made our way down the street to our house.

We found the house in uproar; the car from Hanoi had arrived and Mr Hoan, Mr Sun, Mr Trinh and Xuan were all fussing with Mr Darcy; there was more hugging and shaking hands and everyone was very pleased to meet my friends. Mr Hoan, the inspiring, exceptional, charismatic trainer who had so captivated me when he worked with the preschool teachers in September, would be working with Mr Sun from the Ministry of Education and Training. They would be conducting a Training Session for Grade 1 and 2 teachers in the new curriculum. Both men are in their early fifties, but very different to look at. Mr Hoan is quite short, has thick black hair and wears glasses. His warmth is encapsulated in his wonderful smile. In contrast, Mr Sun is thin and aesthetic looking, with silver hair brushed back from a sculptured face. He looked very sophisticated in his loose jacket, and when he told us that he was also a journalist, somehow his appearance seemed to fit that persona.

The next morning twenty teachers arrived from all the outlying areas. The training was from half past seven in the morning until nine o'clock at night with the obvious breaks. They had come long distances, and one man had travelled for over four hours through the forest and across rivers. His placement was the most isolated, and they all enjoyed meeting at Mrs Mai's guesthouse as it gave them a chance to gossip and exchange experiences before the training. Because I was not required for the day, Lyn, Diana and I took the opportunity to visit Mrs Kim, the preschool teacher in Khe Lac. Mr Trinh drove us there and had to cope with Lyn's short, gasping cries as he had so many near misses with puppies, chickens and all the other livestock that wandered without a care onto the road. They were as horrified as I used to be with the road, but like me they fell in love with the stunning scenery, and about a million photographs were taken of the rice harvest, the San Chi ladies and the children. For the first three kilometres home, on the track where the car cannot go, we were followed back from the school by all the schoolchildren, feeling like three pied pipers.

We left Khe Lac and drove on to a café in Binh Lieu for lunch. Diana's mouth fell open like a flytrap when she saw where Mr Trinh led us. A drunken party was in full flow, and rice wine was being consumed with great gusto at breakneck speed as each person was challenged to drink it down 'in a oner'. It was only eleven thirty. There were chicken bones being gnawed by dogs under the table, and all the men were caressing each other affectionately. We were plonked down next to them. Later a sturdy waitress wearing a red bandanna wiped everything on to the floor, smeared the greasy table with a dubious cloth, popped some toothpicks in the middle, then stood and asked us what we wanted to eat. Fortunately Mr Trinh took care of all that, and somehow steaming bowls of vegetables, spicy omelette, tofu and fish appeared, then finally the rice and clear soup to finish off the meal. It was delicious, although we were more interested in the other table and all the celebrating that was going on, as the dogs crunched the sharp bones at our feet.

Mr Trinh obviously needed some respite from caring for us, so he pointed us towards the market, then sat down outside a shop and started playing cards with the men who were already dealing. Lyn very kindly bought me the velour blanket of my dreams! Bright shades of red, pink and orange flowers, and Chinese characters boldly telling a poem amongst all this colour. She smiled warily as a collection of market women gathered round to help with the bargaining. A deal of VND 60,000 – about £3 – was sealed and lifelong friendships were made.

Clutching our purchases, we had intimate chats about our ages and our children and the texture of our arms, and I was awarded an Alice band as a present, probably for being a soulmate and sharing the same outlandish tastes! As we wandered through the market we saw a Dau girl with her baby at her breast. I think she is the youngest mother I have ever seen; she couldn't have been more than about thirteen and was quite beautiful, with her bald head and red box and beautifully embroidered clothes, with the tiniest baby wearing a Chinese emperor's hat. Later we discussed the injustice of it all. The women have to go through life, from puberty to death, wearing these clothes, and the men just wear the uniform of western shirts, trousers, floppy black hair and plastic shoes. It does vary in different areas, though, as Vietnam has, in fact, fifty-four different ethnic minorities, and countless subdivisions have each developed their own dialects and costumes over the centuries. The Hmong are the most common ethnic group around the northwest mountainous region of Sapa. There, both men and women wear home-dyed indigo clothes made from hemp; the women sport long 'aprons' and embroidered waistcoats over baggy shorts, their hair rolled into turbans; the men wear skullcaps, loose trousers, shirts and long waistcoats with embroidered mandarin collars. There is a wonderful Museum of Ethnology in Hanoi that depicts each group's costumes and culture.

When we got back to Tien Yen we found that Hang had pulled out all the stops for dinner for our visitors and it was spectacular: huge prawns; spicy pork; fresh fish cooked in tomatoes and dill; beef and so many green vegetables; and bowls of steaming rice. Lyn and Diana had brought vodka and presented the three men with cartons of cigarettes, which they smoked just about two at a time. Mr Hoan gave the ladies original Vietnamese paintings and then, of course, we sang 'Santa Lucia', several times, until I taught them

'The Autumn Leaves' and they taught us the Russian song 'Catchusa'.

From the rousing choruses, the mood changed when Mr Son recited a poem he had written about autumn, and hair, and the moon, and new love. It was very deep, philosophical and beautiful. He wrote it out and Xuan translated.

That evening, Lyn and Diana cut, plaited, stitched and gathered all their lifetime's talents into little prince and princess costumes for me to use as enhancers for imaginary role play. One minute there were bits of blue cloth neatly folded, the next little dresses and capes were hanging over chairs. Of course they muttered and complained about 'holiday' and 'not supposed to be working' throughout, but Xuan and I just ignored them and we now have the know-how to pass it on. VSO is all about sharing skills, after all!

Today I had to do a session on story telling with the teachers. I have the advantage of having English, and wanted to demonstrate how frustrating it is to hear words and yet not be able to understand. I told the story of Zaccheus with no visual aids and using a very intimidating manner, so the teachers could perhaps empathise with their children who do not understand the Vietnamese that is used in the classroom. I then retold the story with warmth and body language, using my own drawings in order to illustrate the key characters, and then introduced key words. What was supposed to be a thirty-minute slot turned into an hour and a half as Mr Hoan joined in and added and embellished the theme. When the teachers had illustrated their own story, we asked them to retell it and give it a title. I had to smile as one man decided to make Zaccheus climb the tree to commit suicide because he was so small and bad, and transformed Jesus into a hunter who had just come back from the forest and invited Zaccheus in for a cup of rice wine. Names for the story were 'Finding a Smile' and 'The Painful Story of Life'.

Lyn and Diana left this morning, and already the house seems empty without them; it was just so good to talk. It was wonderful seeing everything anew through their eyes, and the enthusiasm that I felt as I talked to them and showed them my new life reinforced the feelings that I have about working in this beautiful country and the growing sense of pride that I have in the new friends that I have made here.

Tien Yen

13 November 2001

I have been ill and had a fever, and just lay in bed yesterday under a thick Chinese blanket. I was feeling miserable and got such a surprise when Mrs Mai, our neighbour who runs the guesthouse, knocked on my door and brought me broth. After I had eaten she told me to turn over and, using the rim of a rice bowl she rubbed Chinese oil that smelt strongly of eucalyptus and camphor into my back with downward strokes of the bowl. It was soothing and hot, and then she covered me up with the blanket and left me to sleep. I do feel better today, though I am still wearing a fleece and woollen socks.

Mrs Mai came back and taught Hang how to make the soup. I watched as she put pork ribs, potatoes, carrots, onions and fish sauce into a pan and cooked them for ten minutes. She then added one litre of water and left it to simmer for an hour. Just before serving she added chopped spring onions and coriander leaves, then we ate it for lunch.

Outside everyone is in padded jackets and anoraks. Winter must be here; it has rained all day and it certainly feels chilly, though we are lucky as there are parts of Vietnam that have been badly damaged by Hurricane Ling Ling that came from the Philippines.

Tien Yen

15 November 2001

My social life has taken off. I still cannot believe this latest development, and it is so different from my quiet introspective sewing evenings. Every night I take Mr Darcy out for a walk, and the other night I passed a group of matrons all sitting out on the street. They are the ladies who run hotel guesthouses or breakfast businesses, and are generally the middle class of Tien Yen. They called me over and seemed very interested in my shape and kept trying to 'pinch an inch'. They wanted to know how old I was, where I bought my earrings and how much they cost. Just the usual chitchat!

In Vietnam it is very important to know the age of someone as it defines the pronoun necessary for addressing each other in conversation. It would not be respectful to call an older person '*em*' or it might be insulting to address a younger person as '*chi*', so once the age question is established then conversation can take on the proper forms.

Minh, the obvious leader of this group of ladies, invited me to come to her house the following night at nine o'clock, as she had a wheel-like gadget that we would be using for the 'abdominals'. I quickly realised that I was to be a part of Tien Yen's new fitness drive and volunteered to bring a tape of Jane Fonda's aerobics, so we parted with a lot of smiles. The next night, Xuan answered the phone and said, 'Gael, it's for you.' I took the call and heard a very loud voice shout, '*Chi Em* OK!' and then it went dead. That was my signal for the new Keep Fit Class. Xuan volunteered to come with me (for the first time) and we set off.

When we got to Minh's, there was a crowd of ladies sitting on the pavement outside and we were given tiny plastic chairs and sat in the ditch. Great trucks trundled their way past us, and above the sky was black and distant stars twinkled. I wondered what my other friends in Vietnam were doing at that moment. Inside, Minh's husband had been entertaining in the very palatial sitting room. There was a large, ornate three-piece suite, carved and inlaid with mother of pearl, and on the walls a variety of industrial calendars showed girls in different colours of *ao dais.*

The television and VCR were set up for karaoke and the men had the book in front of them with all the song titles. In Vietnamese karaoke, when the selected song comes up, they take the microphone and just belt it out. There seems to be no need or requirement to be able to sing or hold a tune, just a great deal of self-esteem and confidence. I am not sure if they are innate qualities or derived from the beer that is always on hand.

Eventually the women were allowed into this smoky den, but then we were ushered through the spacious sitting room into a tiny back bedroom that was taken up with a huge 'Scottish Castle' four-poster bed. It had navy blue velvet curtains – obviously for privacy – but my goodness it must have been hot.

I counted nine potential keep-fitters and some started on the wheel with great enthusiasm. They knelt on the floor and pushed forward and then had to pull the wheel back towards them and pull themselves upright again. Xuan looked at me and we raised our eyebrows as we both wondered how we were going to do aerobics in this small space. The electrical connection proved a big drama as well, as the VCR plug kept falling out and blue sparks would fly out every time it was pushed back in. After all my previous shocks I was really losing my faith in Vietnamese skills in electrics, especially as I found out that nothing is earthed. Minh's son came and secured the plug into the wall with

Sellotape, and it held just long enough for my first class. I simply could not look at anyone while we jumped and gyrated as I would have dissolved laughing. In the doorway the men had all gathered to have a look before they went back to their own entertainment, which was on full volume. Poor Jane was turned up to the highest I could put her, but it was all we could do to make out what she was shouting about.

We finished the workout with faces the colour of aubergines. Minh made us orange juice then ushered us into the 'great lounge', which had been vacated except for cigarette smoke. She thought we should all have a bit of karaoke to end the evening. So now I am no longer a karaoke virgin, I lost it with good old 'Danny Boy'.

Tien Yen

20 November 2001

Well, it's been all go. I got up at four o'clock this morning and sat out on my balcony draped in my blanket, all set to watch the great Leonides shooting star show. In the paper it was advertised like some forthcoming Disney attraction, with all the stars in the sky putting on a meteorite display. I wasn't sure what to expect but there did seem to be a million shooting stars, so I sang the song about wishing on a star and made wishes on behalf of all my nearest and dearest; there were so many that I ran out of nearest and dearest!

According to today's paper, the best place for viewing was in north China, so perhaps I just saw the tail end and not the major feature. I don't mind as it was quite special; so silent and cold, and the sky was alive.

Today is Teacher's Day, so Xuan and I set off on the bike to celebrate with the teachers at Dong Ngu. I took the helmet off my head and had no time to sort out my coiffure before I was whisked into a crowded hall where Xuan and I watched speeches and songs and flowers being presented. Then, horrors, I had to make a speech with flattened hair (oh the shame) and Xuan translated. The Chief of the Village looked as though he should have been golfing with Bob Hope. He certainly seemed in the same age bracket (around ninety) and had on a very Edward VIII style golfing hat. He got down from the podium and went to sit with his buddies, and I had to laugh as they genuinely looked so out of place in their turn-of-the-century golf clothes. One even had a pair of two-toned shoes.

Lunch was next on the agenda, so we set off to the local restaurant. I smiled at the pretty teachers all dressed in white *ao dais*, cycling with straight backs, their long hair falling under the rim of their conical hats. I had seen pictures of teachers and students in the south of Vietnam dressed this way, so it was good to see our teachers similarly dressed to mark this special day in their calendar.

There were about sixty of us for lunch and the tables were laden with food, so we started selecting different dishes: fish; meat; vegetables; spring rolls. Unfortunately no one got a chance to eat as it is the custom for all the important people like the Headmaster and the Chairman of the People's Committee to circulate first and drink to everyone's health until everyone is blotto. There was so much hand-shaking, hugging and *tram phan tram* (bottoms up – or more literally, one hundred percent). Binh, who was sitting next to me, downed glasses of beer straight every time she was challenged and then kept hugging me and speaking very slowly... she was a hoot.

Interpreter Xuan left me to converse with the teachers in my still rudimentary Vietnamese, went off chattering to another table, then came back all pink and flushed. We had photographs taken, reminiscent of wedding ones, all gathered together with some people kneeling in front. I have a feeling that when they come out it will look as though I have just got married to the Headmaster.

We got back on the bike with tipsy Xuan at the controls and zoomed home. I just shut my eyes tight when anything large loomed out of the dust. We were ready for a siesta to recover, and then had other courtesy visits in the afternoon bringing flowers to other teachers in Tien Yen.

At nine o'clock the phone went as usual, '*Chi Em* OK!' Minh was dressed up in a dark suit, drop earrings and a bobble hat. The Scottish castle bed with thick curtains had been ousted from the back room and placed behind the wall unit that lodges the karaoke machine in the sitting room. I have been told that in the cities karaoke bars are really brothels, so a true crooner has to be discerning where they go. I just hope Minh isn't planning to use the bed and charge by the hour!

New machines have been installed. Minh had ordered two walking machines with body vibrator belts attached, plus a torture gadget for sit-ups, from a catalogue, and these joined the original wheel for the abdominals. Chairs had been placed alongside, and as I sat and waited for a turn on something, I was reminded of being at a dance in the Kyle Hall in the northwest highlands of Scotland. There was the proximity to the action, and yet because you were still seated, you were just an observer and thus apart.

As we waited, the local lads came in to have a look. These were the macho lads, all cloned to the John Travolta-type look – clean and slick, with polished shoes and ironed shirts. One fellow lay back on the special sit-up machine, pinned his feet in the special stirrups and proceeded to do twenty sit-ups, with a cigarette in his mouth that he puffed away at during the whole exercise.

I think we were all secretly relieved when they left and we could get on at our own pace. These women have a definite need for their new gym, as the rolls of fat must come just as easily from a rice diet as a bread and potato one. My needs are more surgical though, for as I put on my war paint in the morning, peering into a tiny compact, I am so aware of the tick-tock of time. In this land where everyone has smooth ivory skins until they suddenly crack like broken porcelain at the tender age of about ninety, it makes poor mortals like me regret the times I laughed too much or squinted, scowled or forgot my sunglasses. Oh tick-tock, tick-tock. Someone stop the clock.

As I sat looking at the stars last night, wishing every few minutes, I just wondered about choices and the whys and wherefores and how life seems to be going by so fast. I pondered whether I should go home, sell my Edinburgh flat and buy a cottage in the country and keep chickens. Maybe I should be like Dorothy and stop jumping over rainbows into other cultures and be happy in my own 'Kansas'. But, as Gabriel Garcia Marquez said in *One Hundred Years of Solitude*, being torn between two cultures is like putting two mirrors face to face and both sets of memories tug and have equal relevance. My earlier childhood memories of the Far East have been compounded with the years I spent in Singapore when I was married, and now I have added another dimension.

I was proud of myself today, being part of the teaching community, not sitting on the chairs looking on but being integrated into the group. It is not good to be alone for too long and, apart from two days with Lyn and Diana, I haven't really spoken to anyone for seven weeks. It does make me melancholy and introspective... not a good combination. All I can say is thank goodness I had the presence of mind to start this quilt. I stitched up a few of the flowers last night, and they look quite beautiful. It just may end up on my bed, one fine day.

Tien Yen

22 November 2001

Visits to schools continue and the harvest is in. Fields are all stubbly, reminiscent of ploughed furrows of my homeland minus the seagulls. It is quite nice during the day when the sun is out and it is warm, but by evening it turns sharply colder. I feel as goggle-eyed as I did in the beginning because in winter the fashions are so eye-catching and eastern. Apart from the chic young things, it seems to be a fashion where anything goes. There are no drab blacks, browns and greys; instead there are jolly reds, oranges and yellows. There are corduroy, velour, acrylic, Adidas, and so many bobble hats that sometimes I wonder if I am not in a ski resort. The casual elegance of these thin bodies in loose jackets and high heels makes them so much more attractive than their summer gear of pyjama-style ensembles.

Sitting on my balcony in the afternoon sun, I cannot believe I was at a school this morning feeling so ashamed of my possum wool socks and sturdy Kicker shoes, fleece and scarf. I sat on a frigid cement floor beside children in ripped cotton shirts, bare feet and rivers of snot coming from their noses. Most were so cold and hungry their eyes were dull.

There's no other way to put it: the young teacher was a bitch from hell. It took all my reserve not to slap her smug face. She knelt on the floor with a stick, which she kept slamming down, and the children cowered in the corner. My first appalled thought was: lion tamer! Xuan and I exchanged glances then moved in very gently and took slates and chalk and started drawing. I kept guiding the teacher's hand away as she automatically tried to rub out a child's tentative attempt at making marks. After a while we saw smiles and felt a little hand rest on our backs or legs;

soon we moved on to paper and felt tips, and eventually hung up the finished portraits. The children were so proud, and I think the teacher saw that there is a better way to communicate. The whole thing is like skating on ice; it is so important not to offend her, and we have to be seen as friends who are supporting her. This morning was, I hope, as positive for her as it was for the children.

Bich is here for a few days and has been off visiting schools in Ba Che district. She and I are going to Mon Cai tomorrow to buy toys for the children in the preschool. We hope to run workshops for making toys out of wood and natural materials, and to utilise the skills that are indigenous to the area... but that is in the future, and at the moment the classrooms are empty, so we are going to buy some blocks and dollies and balls and anything else that is suitable from the large market on the Chinese border.

Mr Darcy is in disgrace. We took him to Phi Guik to visit Mrs Thuy, but the road seemed worse than normal and poor Darcy was sick. Mr Trinh was also sick cleaning up this horrible mess of noodles, so we left a big pile of vomit in the middle of the forest. So that is the end of Mr Darcy being a mascot dog.

We were invited to Mrs Mai's for dinner last night. It was absolutely delicious, and she had gone to so much trouble. We all ate in our jackets and scarves as the temperature had plummeted to near freezing and the houses do not have any heating. It made me think of train stations in the Scottish winter where people huddle around draughty tables trying to keep warm. With so many clothes on, you have to be careful not to spill sauce or soup on to your scarf. We all sat around a circular table laid out with dishes containing prawns, Vietnamese shredded salami, peanuts, grated carrots and cucumber, fresh white noodles and salad leaves. Each person had at hand a pile of papery thin spring roll wrappers. We made parcels of all the ingredients, then dipped them into a bowl made up of fish sauce, vinegar, chilli, garlic, sugar and shredded green papaya. The meal was long, involved and busy, as we each made up little parcels and presented them to each other. Beer was drunk, and I smiled proudly as I offered my lumpy masterpiece to Mrs Mai, who very kindly ate it. Xuan, I am sure, ate about twenty-five and Mr Trinh had about thirty, but who was counting?

After dinner, Bich suggested that we go dancing. She was not interested in the Keep Fit Class, so we all went on the back of a motorbike and found a disco place that had flickering lights, and we danced and drank hot orange juice – really wild. I was amazed at Bich's talents; she is so good at the cha-cha. She and Hiep teamed up and performed for us, then attempted to teach Xuan and me. I fear it will need more than one lesson.

I loved coming home in the blackness, over the bridge into Tien Yen, the black river below and the moon and stars spread out above us. Tonight was fun, but I am feeling so lonely, I sometimes feel so conscious of being the foreigner and just want to go home.

Tien Yen, 25 November 2001

My dear Gerry,

Well well well! The news today is that the real Princess Anne is to visit. And she wants to see our project. Xuan and I are so excited and want to wear ao dais *especially… that is the long silky dress open at the hips and worn over loose trousers. We should look like a right gruesome twosome in our great palace. Anyway, it is not until May so there will be plenty of time to get the duster out before then.*

We are going back to Hanoi on Sunday, so that should be a nice change, and then we are going to Bangkok. I am meeting Sheila there on the Monday for dinner before she flies back to Scotland. When she rang she was full of news of the coming St Andrew's Ball; I had such a twinge of envy as I remembered what fun they used to be in Kota Kinabalu, and how the practices were so serious they were almost religious. Happy days, but they still are… though different.

Love Mum

Hanoi, 26 November 2001

My dear Gerry,

We drove down from Tien Yen today, and as usual I watched the scenery pass and the tree-clad hillsides give way to the Armageddon blackness of the coal sites of Cam Pha and then finally into the teeming madness of Hanoi. I hate it, and hate the stupidity as people try to outdo each other with their characteristic impatience and mindless aggression. Pavements are as unsafe as the roads as motorbikes veer on to the walkways in their bid to get ahead. I just can't stand the traffic and the change of personality that seems to occur when people take to the roads. The government is trying to introduce a bus system to reduce congestion, but still the thousands of motorbikes behave like gnats or stinging insects as they swarm in their desperation to be first.

I came into my room here in the hotel and had a beer, and I am wondering if it is literally possible for your heart to hurt? I feel such pain in my chest and have to squeeze my eyes to stop the tears. I have tried so hard to keep an open mind to cultural differences and remember that it was my choice to come to work here, so I have to understand that I must accept practices that may seem unnatural to what I have been accustomed to in my own country.

As I gazed out of the window of the car today we drove through a small village north of Halong Bay. Mr Trinh slowed and stopped at a railway crossing to let a miniature locomotive with its little box cars full of coal pass by.

I idly looked out at the roadside shops. My eyes finally focused on what was on the pavement just a few metres from the car. There were eight small wire cages, each containing a dog. They were of different sizes and looked scared and cramped and pathetic. Some cages were piled on top of others. It took me a few moments to realise what was in the large plastic laundry bowl in front of these animals. It was a dead dog steeped in boiling water. From where I sat it looked like an Alsatian and it was about to be skinned. *Above the doorway of the wooden shack there was the tell-tale sign:* Thit Cho or *Dog Meat.*

I know, I know. I had heard and even read accounts of this, and had seen a blackened animal that had been barbecued with a blow torch in the market, but when you see them in the process of being killed only a few metres from you, it assaults every sensitivity you possess.

Later…

I met Sam, a fellow NGO worker who is also staying in the hotel, and we had dinner together. He could see I was upset and I blurted out all my feelings of outrage and pain, but was not prepared for what he told me. It is not just Vietnam, but Korea, China, the Philippines and northern Thailand: all are guilty of the cruelty that is involved in the dog meat trade.

He told me that in some countries dogs are tortured prior to killing them as this increases their adrenalin levels and the meat is then considered to be an aphrodisiac. The animals are often clubbed then slowly bled to death, or they can be given electric shocks to the tongue and then finally skinned and torched when they are still alive. Frequently they beat and break the legs first, so the animal is in excruciating pain. And often when dogs are killed, others bark and cry as they hear the ones near them being butchered by slow and primitive means.

My throat was tight and I could feel tears welling as I screwed up my napkin. Sam then went on to tell me about bear bile. I had seen two bear cubs at a restaurant in Halong Bay and, after being reassured that they were not to be eaten, I had just about forgotten the incident. Now I listened in horror at what these animals were forced to endure. Throughout Asia it is believed that the bright green bile, siphoned off from the bear by cruel metal catheters surgically inserted into its gall bladder, is essential in traditional Oriental medicinal concoctions and is useful in treating fever, liver illnesses and sore eyes.

(What is wrong with Optrex for sore eyes, I want to know?)

The bears suffer intolerably in cages no bigger than the size of their own bodies, and can be left to lie confined and alone for up to twenty-two years. The teeth are sawn off and claws removed, and sometimes they are missing limbs as a result of capture in the wild by leg-hold traps. Many have chronic infections caused by the unsanitary surgical procedures used in the implantation of the catheters.

All of this cruelty (the majority of cases are from China) is for a product that can so easily be replaced by natural herbs. Chinese medicine experts have now come up with herbal alternatives to bear bile products, so at last there is a move away from this barbaric procedure. The work of the Animal Watch Organisation has highlighted these facts to the world, and already steps are being taken by humane organisations to rehabilitate some bears and nurse them back to health.

Superstition and tradition will be a huge factor in preventing this progress, for I know that people here in Vietnam will turn to the old remedies when confronted with illnesses as frightening as liver cancer. It is hard to persuade people, who have little hope and little chance of hospital care and surgery, to abandon the belief that a glass of bile wine might offer the elusive cure.

Vietnam has long been involved in trapping and exporting her exotic, rare and domestic animals to China, for these animals have been the foundation of a very lucrative business in both the aphrodisiac and the medicinal market. We can only hope that in the future, with world pressure and with the growing environmental education programmes and increasing medical awareness, demands will decrease, and Vietnam will follow more humanitarian, modern trends.

And as for me, I sipped my Coke but had no appetite. What I had heard just compounded my pain from the sights of the morning. Sometimes it is so hard living here.

Goodnight,
Love Mum

Hanoi

11 December 2001

It's been an educational two weeks, and Tien Yen seems so far away and removed from all the new experiences that I have undergone. Walking around Hanoi I have had time to gather my thoughts and piece together the jumbled jigsaw of days at the SCF office preparing for our trip to Bangkok: whizzing on *xe oms* in order to get pictures laminated; collecting photographs and being involved in meetings; meeting Colm from VSO and getting dressed up to go to the Press Club, then drinking tequila tonic and wobbling on the back of his push-bike at midnight through silent streets to the crazy Apocalypse Night Club, which had a cross section of every type of humanity squashed inside.

Xuan, Bich and I flew to Bangkok and were overwhelmed by the heat and the concrete and the skyscrapers; however, we loved the efficiency of the Skytrain public transport and we joined the millions in their desire to shop, shop, shop. Suddenly we realised it was the run-up to Christmas; Santas and Christmas trees were lit up to the size of the buildings, the sky was glowing, and everywhere we went there were carols and glitter and panic buying. Somehow I had forgotten Christmas this year, for Hanoi is very low key, but I imagine it won't be long before they incorporate Santa into their already long list of celebrations. Bich seemed to think most of her relatives ought to have a present to commemorate 25 December, and I went with her to buy little dolly backpacks and various cuddly toys.

I did have a reflective moment and thought of Edinburgh and the cold, wet streets, the icy wind, the Christmas lights and the shops all glittery in greens and reds with gold and silver stars. It all seemed so far away. I remember years ago, when I felt that all this consumerism was destroying the real Christmas message, I gave an ultimatum to my three children, who were then eleven, nine and six. They had to perform, for their Dad and me, a proper Nativity Play by seven o'clock on Christmas Eve. We had no idea what to expect, but it is something that I think all of us now remember.

We were living in the northwest of Scotland, in a tiny village, in a big stone house that used to be an old manse. All around us were mountains, and in December the light was gone by three in the afternoon; snow showers were frequent and home was somewhere that was warm and where fires burned. Outside the sea crashed onto the beach at the bottom of our garden, and the black silhouettes of the mountains of Skye loomed like a dark presence. In the distance our neighbours' houses were lit up with welcoming pinpricks of light.

Dave and I were invited to sit on the stairs looking down on the huge Christmas tree. It was erratically decorated, and held treasures from all our years together – the first silver foil bells that were made in playschool, the favourite wooden train, all the various baubles and tinsel. The hallway was dark except for the tree lights and one candle. We waited.

Nicko entered with the Bible, and proceeded to read from Matthew Chapter 6. The scene was set for the two superstars, dressed up in all sorts of floaty nighties and scarves, to re-enact that very first story. Natasha, aged six, was a solemn angel as she hovered and delivered her glad tidings, and Gerry was a beautiful Madonna as she held her baby and received her gifts. I can still hear their childish voices as we joined them in singing 'Silent Night', and the tree and the candlelight lit their faces.

The years have whizzed by, and I have the luxury of

daydreaming in the middle of a Bangkok department store. This year I do not feel the need to stress the Christian story, though, for all around me people are doing so much for others, regardless of which faith they follow.

Our workshop comprised a good mixture of nationalities. The raucous chatter of the Chinese and Vietnamese contingent contrasted with the solid calm of the Tibetan girl from Lhasa, who brought A4 pictures of her schools and children, all framed by snowy mountains and scenes of yak buying. She told us of the serious contracts that were written in beautiful, indecipherable script for the school's purchase of one black, hairy yak. All the produce, the milk, butter and cheese, can then be sold to buy books and pencils and other school necessities.

So different from Bich's idea. She suggested that our schools should raise rabbits and the children should learn to care for them. I was nodding and smiling and thinking of Flopsy and Mopsy, then she went on to say the meat would be a good supplement to their diet! Oh God… I think I am just too naïve.

The Indonesian team brought stories of their often traumatised children, who are subject to war and conflict. The two ladies from Laos, with names that were so long and unpronounceable compared to the one-syllable names of the Vietnamese, were happy with the progress in their work, which included devising special activities for children with handicaps and learning difficulties. Because their previous programme was so successful, they were being encouraged to expand to further regions in Laos.

Devising games and activities for such a huge cross-section of children was our task. Our Vietnamese contribution was story-telling, and we used a traditional folk legend about An Tiem who, after being banished to an island by a jealous King, saw a white pheasant drop six seeds. He and his wife gathered and planted the seeds and watched them grow into watermelons, and soon their island retreat became famous for the fruit.

Our time in Bangkok coincided with the King's birthday, a national holiday, so we continued the workshop at the home of one of the Thai SCF team, Amanda. It was a perfect oasis, and we sat around a swimming pool set in a garden that could have been Eden. There were frangipani trees, orchids, bougainvillaea and lotus, and somehow the city noises were lost.

During lunch (a Thai curry, of course), I listened to Xuan and the Chinese girls chatting about boys and the elusiveness of Mr Right, and then Lu Hong went on to tell of the problems that can come after you find him, particularly in China. She and her husband live in Kunming, in Yunun Province, and have to share a small flat with another couple. Another difficulty is that the apartment is on the seventh floor, with no lift. After the allotted one baby appeared to each couple, they would put up notices: 'Please don't wash dishes – baby sleeping!' One advantage of having an in-house sibling, especially in a country where more than one baby is frowned upon, is that both children have a friend and learn all the social skills of having to share and take turns.

I went to see the film Harry Potter. Bangkok is wonderful; so western, with beautiful plush modern cinema complexes. Apart from standing in the dark for the National Anthem, and sitting through hours of forthcoming attractions, I loved the film, but sniffed all the way back to the hotel because it was filmed in Scotland and it made me want to go home. Maybe it was the Christmas theme, but I went through a sad patch for a couple of days and I just wanted to leave. At the airport on the way back to Hanoi, I saw a British Airways stewardess strutting briskly and I had to fight the urge to throw myself at her feet and let her drag me to the plane.

At the workshop we met an English woman who was out running a course on gender issues. She joined Bich, Xuan and I on our sightseeing expeditions to temples, *klongs* (canals) and palaces. On the Saturday night we decided to go and see a sex show, and all I can say is that now we know all about ping-pong balls, razor blades, strings of flowers and bells. There were also some very amazing vaginal writing and drawing techniques, and a unique trick with a banana. The taxi driver was just so enthusiastic; he nearly went off the road turning round to tell us all the new tricks we would learn! The highlight was the full sex act, which was very polished and professional but so cold and lacking in emotion. Mind you, considering the man had to do it every night every half hour from nine o'clock until one o'clock, I suppose it's a miracle that he could do it at all!

We were sitting near the bar, and the girls would come off the little stage where they had been writhing against poles and sit next to me (completely naked). I was surprised at how sexless they were; no busts or waists and very solid bodies, and they were so bored. I am not, however, denying their talents. I was chatting to them and asking how the razor blades trick was done, and what their hours were, and how old they were, and did they take turns to do the sex act, so next year I just may have a new technique for blowing out the birthday candles! Oh come back, Tien Yen, all is forgiven!

Tomorrow we drive back up north. It is so cold and it feels worse because it is raining, but I bought a hot water bottle and I have the Chinese blanket, and both Xuan and I are looking forward to seeing Mr Darcy. We bought him a red collar, so he will be very smart.

Anne, from London, and Bill, the country director of SCF, are visiting later this week, so hopefully the weather will improve and they will see a few of our schools.

Tien Yen, 14 December 2001

My dear Gerry,

I don't know what has gone wrong, but Xuan is locked up in some private world of her own, where she is moody and angry about something but refuses to talk. I have asked her but she sits and cuts me dead or goes up to her room, so now the days are even longer and it rains and I am still so homesick and keep doubting my ability to stay on here. It is so isolated and I am so lonely and I just miss you all and I have no one to talk to.

It's funny how, if you have someone to share a problem with, it somehow doesn't seem so huge anymore, but when you are alone things grow and grow. It is humiliating when we sit and eat and she refuses to talk to me and I don't know why.

Love Mum

Tien Yen, 15 December 2001

Dear Gerry,

It has been a day from hell. I have packed all my possessions into the suitcases and somehow have got them all zipped up. My room is as bleak as I remember it when I first saw it. Bill and Anne have arrived and I feel terrible. I don't understand what has gone wrong and what I have done to upset Xuan so much. All I know is that I want to leave – the posting is lonely enough as it is, life is too short, and I just want to go home.

Later...

Bill has been the peacemaker and has persuaded me to stay on and try and resolve things. I am sure he is right, and things will regain their balance. But I am afraid, for being with Bill and Anne and talking freely and verbalising all my worries and pent up feeling of loneliness has been wonderful, but it is short-term, and I know they will have to go and my real life will have to resume. I just pray that Xuan and I will be able to build the bridges.

Anne and I went and drank beer at a Bia Hoi, and we nearly froze to death; the temperature is around 3°C.

Love Mum

Tien Yen

17 December 2001

We set off this morning to visit the Directors of Education and the Chairman of the People's Committee in Binh Lieu and Ba Che districts. Everyone was on his or her best behaviour, it was very formal and people stood up before they spoke. We all sat around a large boardroom table in the offices in Ba Che, drinking steaming glasses of strawberry tea to keep us warm. Everyone kept on their jackets and scarves, and the ladies wore an assortment of hats. One was particularly eye-catching, a black cloche kept on with the most gigantic hatpin topped with a huge pearl. I would say she was the most formal, as the other ladies just sported woolly little numbers, which made me think of winter sports.

As we drove up into the mountains of Binh Lieu we passed so many fashions, and the colours just all ran together. Old ladies draped shawls around their faces and tied them on the top of their heads as though they were suffering from toothache. Men had Moscow ear-warmer specials and wore greatcoats; you would think they had just fallen out of Napoleon's army. Binh Lieu itself was bleak though, the rice husks brown, the fields wintry, and just lonely wisps of smoke escaping from the houses. People squatted in their doorways covered in jackets and scarves but their feet were bare.

The highlight of the day was the meeting with the Chairman of the People's Committee in Binh Lieu. This was housed in the grandest, most spacious pink and white Tara-like mansion. The boardroom table was the height of elegance and the chairs were so new they still had the cellophane on (and the price). The Chairman himself was a diminutive man with a very large ring. I thought we might all have to kneel and kiss it! The meeting went well, with Bill speaking and Bich translating, and we heard from the Chairman of the appalling poverty in the area, and how they were pleading for more SCF intervention and help. Only about forty-two percent of the people earn VND 80,000 a month; about £4. They could see the need for education in the ethnic minority groups and how positive the SCF work in Tien Yen district has been, and so want to emulate it.

We drove back, all of us lost in our own thoughts, and I couldn't help thinking of the ripple in the pond. The philosophy that has been put into action in Tien Yen is now sending little waves of interest into the surrounding districts. I just hope these powerful men with beautiful committee rooms can meet the charity groups halfway, and then perhaps all our efforts will have a chance to be sustained.

Later that night Hang provided the spring rolls, squid and pork, and the local education team came to eat and drink with us. It was a wonderful party, with beer drinking challenges met and friendships forged. The end result was a mass exodus to Minh's karaoke, where foreigners v Vietnamese dominated the large sitting room. All this took place whilst the ladies of the Keep Fit worked out regardless in the back room.

Everyone went back to Hanoi the next day, and I was left alone with Hang and Mr Darcy. I took him for walks and sewed my quilt. The next few days were the same. There was no one to talk to; Xuan had gone, and I didn't know how anything was going to be resolved. I was cold and so, so sad.

A new translator has been sent up, and Xuan continues not to speak. Unhappiness is exhausting. The pain seems to grip your heart.

We have visited schools and the new translator, not

understanding what I am trying to do, contradicts me in front of the teacher. I am not in the frame of mind to cope with anything at the moment. I just bury my head and sew.

We revisited Dong Hong and filmed Mui showing how she now uses groups and has children working at different activities. We watched her teaching vocabulary through drawings and Plasticine models. We filmed her telling a story with all the children around her, using simple pictures to illustrate her words. It was very effective, and it will be a useful aid for the next group training session.

Xuan and I worked together, and we were briefly reconciled through our understanding of what we hoped to achieve. Perhaps the bridge can be rebuilt. As we walked back to the main road where we were to meet Mr Trinh, the sky was growing dark and the rice fields were bleak. It was cold, and yet the verges at the sides of the road still had lush forest vegetation. It seemed odd to see banana trees look so green in the middle of winter.

Hanoi

21 December 2001

Last night I gave everyone a Christmas present and sang 'Jingle Bells' and 'Silent Night', then we had some beer and everyone seemed a little happier. Today we packed up, said goodbye to Hang, piled into the car and set off for Hanoi. Mr Darcy came too, and he behaved beautifully – he wasn't sick once! He will stay with Xuan over the holiday period, and will ride around the city on her motorbike.

I got the most wonderful surprise… two friends who are doing VSO work in the Maldives had arrived in Hanoi and were booked into the same hotel as me. I wasn't to be alone for Christmas after all, and seeing Rob and Barbara after all these months was just the best of presents.

Hanoi
23 December 2001

Last night we went to the VSO Christmas Party, where we drank wine and ate curry and I met up with friends that I hadn't seen for months. Somehow just being with others made me feel human again, and it was just so good to laugh and be silly and totally relax.

Hanoi

27 December 2001

As I write this I am surrounded by cloth, the ethnic stitching on indigo-dyed fabric that makes up the clothes of the Hmong people of the high mountainous regions of the northwest. When I use my tablecloth, I shall remember their faces and their constant nagging, 'You buy from me, not from her,' and, 'Why you buy from her and no buy from me? OK no photo.' Oh God! Tourism can be such a pain.

Christmas was spent in Sapa, about forty kilometres from Lao Cai, one of the major border crossings to China in the northwest. We knew that we had almost arrived as we began the ascent up the tortuous mountain road that winds round valleys and passes minority villages and rice fields before climbing to the pine-treed environs of the village.

Sapa sits like an Austrian ski resort, surrounded by huge mountains, the highest being Phan Si Pang (3,143m). Everyone told me that Sapa sits in a bowl of mist for five months of the year and that I would not see much but, on the morning of Christmas Eve, I pulled back my curtain and felt like Heidi. There was a glistening wall of rocky mountain, blue sky and sunshine, but it was freezing, only about 2°C.

Rob, Barbara and I had hired a Russian jeep in Hanoi, complete with driver, and had suffered the bone-crunching ten-hour journey of three hundred and thirty kilometres. We arrived in the dark and, though exhausted, we felt it was worth it as we'd passed through some stunning scenery. It had given Rob and Barbara the chance to see much more of rural Vietnam than if they'd taken the overnight sleeper train that was the alternative.

We checked into the Auberge Inn and, after supper, we retired to our rooms and found a roaring fire burning. I stepped onto the terrace of the hotel and looked out on a picture postcard. I felt the silence and the blackness; the stars were bright and the sky was clear, everything seemed to glitter in a frosty expectation. Was I really in Vietnam?

On Christmas Eve we walked and walked, past pine trees arm-in-arm with bamboo, past pot-bellied pink and black pigs. We went off the beaten track, down, down, down into the valleys of man-made sculpted rice fields, which rose in great whorls up the sides of the hills. We had left the hotel in the morning wearing five layers of clothes, but by eleven o'clock we found we had to tie them round our waists as the sun was so hot. Our noses got burnt by the unexpected sunshine. As we walked we met children and old ladies who greeted us with the persistent chorus of, 'You buy from me.' We crossed rivers and got lost in pine forests and ended up in a Hmong village where everyone had purple hands.

I had noticed rosaries around the girls' necks, tangled up with silver torques and jazzy earrings, and then I saw why. A simple wooden building functioned as their church and we were invited inside; it had the same cool, dry feeling and expectant quiet of any European cathedral. To the right of the altar was the Nativity, all beautifully decorated with bamboo and fronds and mosses. The manger was simple and the atmosphere was hushed. Unconsciously the three of us bowed our heads, and for a few minutes forgot where we were. We came outside to the harsh reality: 'Why you no buy from me?'

That night we did visit the Catholic church in Sapa, but we did not recognise any of the traditional carols. It would seem that neither did anyone else, as the teacher or priest had a stick and blackboard and was shouting to the children in the front, and some wild Vietnamese dirge was being learnt. The three of us cowered on a pew, wondering what form the service would take. To my right, as I gazed about, I got such a jolt and thought I had stepped into a scene from a thriller movie or a nightmare. There was a dad holding his little girl on his hip, and she had on a Halloween Santa mask. It was not the gentle, jovial face I normally associate with Santa; instead I felt quite scared.

We decided to leave and made our way down the aisle to the small door at the rear; it was full of young lads all peering inside. It made me smile; the only things missing were the cans of lager... we could have been anywhere.

On Christmas day, we were given a grand tour of the wonderful garden that the owner had carved into the rock above the hotel, each little nook and cranny planted with every kind of flower imaginable. We were amazed to find that he orders all his seeds from the Thompson and Morgan Seed Catalogue. All his care and love has been rewarded because he has the most beautiful collection of flowers and his setting is truly unique.

We made our way through Sapa's crowds of tiny Hmong in their indigo outfits, and the more regal Dao, crowned by their bejewelled red turbans. We visited waterfalls and villages, and by evening we were ready to join the rest of the world in the traditional feasting ritual. First we drank champagne around the brazier in the hotel's dining room, then we went up to the very classy Victoria Hotel for the most fabulous Christmas buffet. Chris, another VSO whom I had come out with and whom Rob and Barbara had met in Birmingham, joined us for dinner.

The return to Hanoi was sad for me, as I knew that my friends would have to leave and return to their posts in the Maldives, and I was not looking forward to being alone again. The thought of Tien Yen and the months ahead loomed large and dark as a thundercloud. I wandered the streets, wrote emails home and read books. I was invited to drink mulled wine with Bill and his family, and then Xuan

Tien Yen

Future preschool classroom

Chicken for lunch

It's warmer out than in

Learning with slates and stones

Self-portrait

Mother and daughter on the field

Child drawing

The joy of reading

Going to school

The new bridge

Inside class

Teacher training

Everybody wants to see

What's going on in there?

Dao lady

Donating clothes to preschool children

Liz and Agneta with my quilt

Feeding the bear at Ba Vi

Banyan tree in Hanoi

brought Mr Darcy to my hotel and we drank tea and talked and her eyes were warm; I felt there might be a glimmer of hope that we could put all the unpleasantness behind us. With Mr Darcy at our feet and the cups of Lipton tea in front of us, it all felt so normal, and she laughed as she described driving around town with Mr Darcy on the floor of her motorbike. He just loves it all, especially the walks in Lenin Park.

I was afraid to destroy the atmosphere but couldn't help asking Xuan why she had retreated behind her wall of silence. Cultural differences are sometimes barely noticeable because we share a common objective in our work and daily lives, and I think it was our sense of humour and our ability to giggle that had created the strong bond between us. Xuan explained that in Bangkok the situation had changed as Bich entered the equation, and the fine balance was tipped as she tried to ally herself with both Xuan and myself. As a result Bich had belittled Xuan's confidence and her status as the main Project Officer, and so Xuan came to resent me. The link between us, that I thought was as strong and secure as a steel chain, was in fact as fragile and as silky as gossamer webs in the wind.

Now that I had found out what was wrong, I knew we could rebuild our relationship and both our jobs would receive equal respect and recognition. We were lucky, and the friendship that we had shared was strong enough to counter the eastern 'loss of face' that she felt she had suffered. Living together is always difficult when misunderstandings occur and, like anywhere, war persists when the talking breaks down.

The New Year is just around the corner, a time for resolutions, and who knows what it will bring? It is to be the Year of the Horse in the lunar calendar, so perhaps I should ride ahead with optimism.

Balcony, Hang Gai Street, Hanoi
July 2002

Serendipity is wonderful, and I am told there is no meeting without a purpose. It isn't until later that you can evaluate the role a particular person has played in your life. Richard attaches no importance to the liaison that he shared with me during the first six months of 2002. He did not feel deeply for me, and saw the relationship as a complication to his already complicated life. He viewed the early episodes as single moments in time, with no significance, and I was expected to feel the same. I think I probably did at the beginning, but I grew fond of him and just loved the times we shared. Even now, nothing seems the same without him. I didn't want to lose the magic that happened only when he was there.

We met at Christmas at the VSO party. He was stretched out on a sofa drinking red wine, Leonard Cohen was playing and people were eating curry. I had met him before briefly, and, although he was working as an English teacher in a Teachers' Training College in Quang Ninh, our paths had not really crossed. His time as a volunteer was drawing to a close, as his contract was due to end in February. We arranged to have dinner.

He was tall, with brown hair, glasses and green eyes. He wore a black shirt and was in his late forties, though, once I knew him, his age seemed a total lie... he was a true Peter Pan. When he talked he made everything else appear less important, his trials and tribulations made my loneliness seem so insignificant. 'How can you possibly be sad when you can buy ice cream?' His accounts of bus journeys from hell or being locked out of his house and losing his wallet seemed so much more worthy of tears than my days of silence. Richard had the deadpan face of the true raconteur, and his stories would rattle on with all the drama of a disaster movie. Only the smile and the laughing eyes would reassure you that the listener should take most of it with a pinch of salt.

None of the photographs I have seem to portray his sense of fun. They are like the images he wanted to project as his truth. Looking at him now, in pictures framed in an album, I have to close my eyes and conjure up his deep sighs, his black moods and melancholy, his kindness and his infectious laugh.

Hanoi

2 January 2002

Four days, is that all it's been? Four days and I can't stop smiling; inside I feel warm and happy. I never expected to feel like this again. Hanoi has become Richard. The West Lake, the Water Puppets, the pagoda where we saw a bee hive high in the branch of a nearby frangipani tree. The streets of the Old Quarter, and so many stairs. We had to climb stairs everywhere we went, rickety ones, wrought iron ones, spiral and fire escapes. We seemed to spend the time above the world in the leaf canopy, there were trees everywhere. We ate meals, sat in bars, drank beer and rice wine, but the best bits were the cyclo drives and the walks in the dark shadowy streets, so beautiful and silent; the moon was full. We kissed on a street corner and that was the beginning of the nights. Now I miss him. Life will go on, and we shall see each other again, but for now I just want to preserve the four days of magic.

I remember him as he marched through the traffic, regardless, expecting me to follow, never even looking to see if I was still alive. We drank champagne at a wrought iron table on New Year's Eve, then went to Minh's and met friends and sang 'Auld Lang Syne' by Hoan Kiem Lake and I lost my purple scarf.

The woozy, fizzy feeling of eating Eggs Benedict yesterday on the first day of January 2002, then later drinking gin in the sun, looking down from our fourth floor café, balloons floating high above Hoan Kiem Lake. Hanoi was quiet, subdued and, like cities everywhere in the world, most of the population was still asleep.

We exchanged slow, shy, lazy smiles, then said goodbye.

Tien Yen, 5 January 2002

My dear Gerry,

We eventually got back to Tien Yen. The house is so cold, but Hang had cooked up a lovely meal, and, with my new hot water bottle and thick blanket and woollen socks, I should be OK.

It is all go here again, as forty teachers have come for training but there's no Mr Hoan this time, only Hoa, Oanh and Giang. I have been busy, so have had little time to be introspective, and I still have a warm inner glow from my New Year in Hanoi.

Mo, the translator, is making things awkward as she is unwilling to translate and keeps challenging my ideas. I don't think she understands her role, and perhaps she and I do not have natural chemistry, but so far I am winning and the local teachers are growing in confidence. Such a contrast to last September, when the same trainers from the Ministry just dismissed them. 'They can't do it,' they said, 'they don't understand.' They are now amazed at these girls' natural talents.

I had to eat alone this evening as Bich told me that they would be eating a special Vietnamese dish. It was dog. I couldn't believe that they would do that in our home as I thought it was a speciality that you went to a restaurant for. No doubt they gave the bones and scraps to Mr Darcy. The other thing that is annoying me is the public address system that, at about five o'clock every morning, plays rousing music and broadcasts local news and current affairs; it goes on and on, punctuated with operatic singers. I am harbouring evil terrorist thoughts, devising ways of blowing up the loudspeaker system that blots the skyline.

I am also probably hyped up with nerves as Agneta and the London VSO boss, Liz, arrived in the afternoon, just as I had launched into a drama lesson with the teachers. We were acting out 'The Grateful Birds', and the teachers just shone with enthusiasm as they acted their way around the room. I had the odd feeling that I was doing a 'crit' lesson from my college days. Later Liz and Agneta saw my room, then met Bich and all the assembled multitudes for dinner. They had to duck as the bats flew about the room whilst we ate our meal. They visited the quirky bathroom, and eyebrows were raised when I told them that Princess Anne was to be visiting. I remember the first time I had a shower; the shower head was awkwardly placed half over the wash basin. I dropped the soap and followed it as it slid across the floor and into the drain outlet. As I retrieved the soap, I was appalled to find that it had accumulated a black pubic wig!

Around eight o'clock that evening we went to visit my good friend Minh, the Keep Fit Queen, and we were all stunned when she showed us her plans. The end wall of the Keep Fit room is to be knocked down and the room extended to create a space for me to run the aerobic class, while the existing area will have all the machines. Agneta and I just looked at each other and burst out laughing. Apparently the new room will be ready in four days. Then Minh linked arms with us and propelled us to the Post Office. We climbed stairs, followed by six young men, and came into an imposing ballroom with chandeliers. By this stage we were totally gobsmacked, but then it all became clear; this was the new class for ballroom dancing.

The three of us felt very creased and crumpled, as well as gauche and left-footed, for the teacher was so slick. In his pale pink, shiny shirt, he reminded me of a Spanish bullfighter. The young men that had gathered inside were also spruce and smart. The teacher demonstrated his proficiency, dramatically gliding and clicking his heels, his arms held at shoulder height, bent at the elbow. He and the music evoked images of some exotic Latin bar – but perhaps not, for this room was too light for a sultry Antonio, it had more of a feel of the TV programme 'Come Dancing'.

Well, there we were in socks and sandals (not sexy) practising the tango (which is potentially very sexy) up and down this glittering room on a Tuesday night, watched over by a huge white bust of Ho Chi Minh. Liz, Agneta, Minh and Gael. Minh, naturally, was wearing her bobble hat.

My partner and I held each other very gingerly and stared at our feet. There was no grand passion. We were just very proud to make it the length of the room, heads bent, staring at our feet and counting mot, hai, ba, bon! At about nine we left, feeling a little more confident and dreaming of net dresses with numbers on our back, cha cha cha!

We walked round the town and ended up chatting. Agneta and I didn't really notice that we were in the middle of the road, with motorbikes whizzing round us as if we were traffic cones. Liz, having come straight from London, was horrified. Both agreed that, for my own sanity, I needed to change my living quarters. Maybe if I have a little more privacy I shall be able to keep a better perspective of the job.

Lately, I have been having serious thoughts of applying to the International School in Hanoi. I find I cannot cope with the isolation, and small things seem to grow out of proportion. When I do have time with other westerners, it makes it more difficult to settle again… maybe I am just not cut out for this way of life. I do like the teachers and the children, and I just feel so guilty for thinking of leaving.

Lots of love, Mum

Hong Gai City
9 January 2002

Christmas is over, and the New Year has begun. I have decided to be positive and optimistic, yet again. The decorations are down throughout most of the world but, here in Hong Gai City, I am sitting in a café listening to 'The First Noel' playing so sweetly.

The teacher training ended with karaoke and dancing, and, as I walked home with Oanh and Hoa under the stars, I continued to hum 'You are always on my mind'. I felt very happy and have probably lost about another trillion brain cells after all the beer we drank as we bonded the night away. I have become good friends with these ladies and the other staff from the Ministry of Education, and we work well together.

It was very strange this morning when I took Agneta and Liz to meet Mr Thuy, the Director of Education for Tien Yen district, with Xuan doing all the formal translating. Everything was so serious, using proper courtesy phrases, and just once I caught his eye and saw the tiny flicker of a smile. Was this the same man with whom I had been drinking *tram phan tram* the other night, who had shouted 'Gael *oi!*' and dragged me out to his motorbike so we could zoom around the streets to the karaoke bar to sing silly drunken duets?

I have regained my equilibrium these last few days. I realise it's not the big things that bring you down and makes you despair, it's more like the mighty oak being destroyed by all the millions of biting insects that needle into the bark. Personality and culture clashes, and living in a close environment with no privacy are all day-to-day issues, and eventually small irritations build up until all tolerance is eroded.

I came down as far as Hong Gai City with the SCF car and felt quite alone when Mr Trinh dropped me off and the white Landcruiser sped away. Still, it is nice to explore another place and the scenery is awesome. All along the seafront great monoliths of rock rise out of the sea, and the harbour is full of every type of boat, from big cruise ships to industrial cargo carriers, with the little houseboats and sampans filling up all the in-between spaces. I watched two boys perched on the branches of a flame tree, and one was going through the other's hair, presumably looking for bugs. We humans don't seem to have progressed much from the characteristics of our primate relations.

Today I am going to meet Richard.

Tien Yen

16 January 2002

When I think of Richard I smile, when I hear his voice I smile, and nearly the whole time I am with him I laugh. He is funny and silly, vulnerable and charming. We met in Hong Gai City and spent the afternoon climbing Poet's Mountain. The entrance to the almost vertical path was hidden behind some filthy shacks, a few dubious steps off the street.

We picked our way through piles of rubbish, discarded needles and condoms, and passed some horrid dogs that sounded very threatening and far too close. Eventually we got out of the area that humans have defiled, and as we climbed up and úp, the whole panorama started to unfold. Fringed by tall pampas-style grasses, we looked down on Halong Bay and saw the sea, way below, with all its mountains interspersed, as though the great giant of legend had left behind stray beads from its necklace. Baby boats looked almost leisurely from this height, belying the industrious nature of the fishermen. Huge birds floated and swooped in shades of black and tan. We took photos from the top, leaning against the plinth where the hammer and sickle flag fluttered in the wind, and gazed about but we found no poetry from the King who was supposed to have left his thoughts etched in the rock way back in the eighth century.

Coming down from the mountain we felt the chill and realised we were still in winter. We wrapped up in jackets, put on our backpacks, and set off on the motorbike through the filthy coal towns of Cam Pha. I had images of coal dust swirling as I pressed my mouth into Richard's jacket as protection from the black puffs of the exhaust fumes from trucks and lorries. We ended up at the ferry to Van Don

Island looking as though we had both come down a chimney. We asked a shopkeeper if we could wash our faces, so we were led through an alleyway and given a cloth and some water in a red plastic basin; two little girls watched us as we tried to wipe the dirt from around our mouths and eyes.

Then we sailed away to the most beautiful island, a haven with crazy mountains that jut straight up into the sky in knife shapes. It is the largest of about three thousand islands that make up Halong Bay. It was dark when we arrived and we booked into a hotel in the most perfect spot above the pier. We had a balcony that overlooked sampans, fishing boats and street vendors. That night we stood and gazed at the dark, looming shapes of the mountains and the odd lights that dotted the houseboats moored offshore. Downstairs in the restaurant we drank cheap vodka, ate enough for twelve people and watched the street dramas that occurred as we lazily gazed about and talked.

The next day we took off on the motorbike to explore the island. I laughed as Richard called *'ciao em'* or 'hello' to all the children, and we zoomed through tunnels, over rivers, through villages and walked in a silent bamboo forest.

Back at the hotel we relaxed; it was calm and, as the sun set, we sat on our balcony and drank vodka and watched scenes of pigs being unloaded from a boat and being squashed without any dignity into a cyclo. We could hear the frantic squealing all the way up the street as the driver placidly cycled along. We saw fish being dispersed into carts on the quay and being transported to shops and restaurants.

Being totally anaesthetised by the vodka, I felt this was the night I should try snake wine. We ventured out into the street and found a noisy restaurant full of tanks with live fish and crabs, which we were requested to choose from. As we waited we befriended a large black dog, and then Richard ordered a beer and I ordered the 'special' drink. I was upstanding as I downed a glass, and managed not to be sick even though I found two scales in my mouth. Later, as I left the restaurant, I looked at the great flagon on the counter and saw the large assortment of cobras and stripy snakes coiled in the liquid. Oh God. I just hoped my body would absorb all the great medicinal properties that people believe you should expect when you drink reptiles, bats, birds or rats that have been allowed to ferment and decompose in the rice wine.

We ended up at a huge karaoke bar with a stage. I sang 'Those Were The Days', and I still laugh when I remember being presented with roses, just as though I was Princess Anne. Richard was hopping with jealousy because his song didn't come up, so he muttered all the way back and sat on the baby chair on our balcony, smashing it and nearly breaking his coccyx... then sat on the other and broke that too. This time he was howling 'Don't Move Me', and I had visions of us getting him down the winding staircase on the back of a door. All was well by the next morning, and we hid the evidence of the bottles and broken furniture, left the room with the debris of dead roses, cheap vodka and filthy footprints, and took off in a pile of dust. Perhaps the owners would think a rock band had been staying!

We visited the beautiful Tiger Pagoda in Cam Pha, looking calm and relaxed as we lit our incense sticks and prayed, then we zoomed up the road to Tien Yen, breathing the lovely fresh air. Richard inspected the town, the house and Mr Darcy, and then we drove to the sea at Mui Chua and lay on a rock in the sun like lizards; I lazily traced patterns on the inside of his arm and he slept.

Life has returned to school visits and working in the office. It is funny how only two days has changed my perspective and suddenly I don't feel so alone. I can cope knowing that I have something to look forward to, that sometimes the telephone will ring and it will be Richard.

Tien Yen

15 January 2002

I wonder if a crystal ball could have predicted my way of life this time last year? In January I had not given VSO a thought for I was totally involved in Edinburgh school life, my drama club and my friends. I remember dressing to go and see La Boheme, wearing a beautiful new black jacket. It was the time when our drama club performed throughout the city a play about the poet Robert Burns. I spent those evenings dressed in an eighteenth-century costume, complete with mop hat and shawl, and sang 'Flow Gently Sweet Afton' as my particular contribution to the life of the poet.

There was a lot of snow and the pavements were death traps of compacted ice. Edinburgh Council has very thoughtfully put handrails along the side of some of the pavements, especially going down from the castle to the New Town, and it has become a saying that, after a boozy night out, it is customary to 'go home by rail'.

I am still in a mellow frame of mind after New Year in Hanoi, and feel as though I am floating a little above reality, so the journey to Phai Guic yesterday didn't faze me too much. The road is so bad that the journey resembles a ride on a bucking bronco and, even though you are belted in, you still can get your head violently thumped against the window as the car lurches from one pothole to the next major crevasse. The lady doctor and nurse came with us to record all the preschool children's weights and heights, listen to chests and give them worming tablets. At each school they dressed up in their professional white coats and wore very tall, awe-inspiring hats.

In Phai Guic I observed the class of Mrs Thuy of

cinnamon fame and was so impressed. Mrs Thuy has become a superstar. She is a natural teacher and has absorbed everything from the training. Her classroom is well organised, the children's work is displayed at their level, and they were absorbed making Plasticine models and drawing pictures of trees. She had brought in large and small sticks of bamboo and wide and narrow leaves for her maths lesson to make the concepts more real for her class. She previously had concerns for a boy who refused to talk, and mentioned this to his mother. The result was terrible: the mother locked her child in with the buffalo for two days and two nights as punishment. When I asked about him now, she just shrugged and said that he speaks a little.

Mrs Thuy herself has changed. She has a short snazzy haircut, and very large platform shoes, and plans to buy a motorbike with the money from the next cinnamon harvest. She is obviously enjoying her new status.

In all, we visited four schools in the district, but a lot of children were off with measles, and those who were there wore only thin shirts without buttons and had bare feet. The snotty nose was universal.

After I'd observed the class and the doctor had finished her examinations, we waited outside the school for the paperwork to be done. I idly watched a gang of San Chi ladies manually removing earth and transporting it in baskets hung from a pole across their shoulders, their broad, bare feet padding to and fro as they dug and shovelled and carried. Men stood about smoking their cigarettes – they were, of course, the overseers of this new playground in the making. It would be most unseemly for them to get their long fingernails dirty. They can drink as many virility enhancing potions in their rice wine as they like, but our cultures would clash if we were to explain to them our definition of the word 'manly'. Women certainly have to do much of the manual labour as well as cook and care for the family. But they seem to be rewarded for all this drudgery, as they are revered and seen as the pillars of society, the central beam that upholds the home, so their strength is recognised as not only being physical but psychological.

I remember sitting outside this school last September when Mr Trinh bought a chicken from a San Chi lady with a purple umbrella. As I was reflecting on how the rice fields were now so bleak in contrast to that hot, sticky, green time, a crazy lady with a huge hunting knife suddenly came running into the playing area shouting wildly. I raised my eyebrows so high that I am sure you could have seen the whites of my eyes. The teachers just laughed and said she was mad. I could see that quite clearly, but I have memories of the slaughter of children in a school in Dunblane. They said that gunman was mad too.

We stopped for lunch at the school in Khe Quang and, to be sociable, we had some tea first in the teachers' room. Beautiful San Chi girls came to smile at us with their gold teeth gleaming and their tiny babies slung on their backs, all protected from the sun by the inevitable conical hat.

As I squatted on my tiny red plastic chair, the doctor and nurse sprawled on one of the teacher's beds. Mr Trinh flopped on another. I felt so proper, sitting primly, sipping my tea, as the others lay with their legs akimbo picking their toes. The room was filthy, full of dust, dirt, rubbish and a motorbike. Newspapers were stuck to the walls and wire was strung across the room for washing.

Standards in this school were poor. Teachers were lazy but, because they were miles from anywhere, surrounded by forest, rice and cinnamon plantations and the usual walls of bamboo, maybe they were all just concentrating on breeding. There were babies, puppies, piglets and chickens everywhere.

We moved into the Grade 4 classroom with its old-fashioned wooden desks set out in rigid rows, and closed the shutters and door to give us privacy from the prying eyes of the children. We ate bread, compressed pork and tangerines (Hang's favourite picnic package for us) and drank La Vie bottled water while I wondered what we would do to fill in the lunch hour. It all became clear when the doctor just stretched out on top of a row of desks, then the nurse did the same, and Xuan and Mo settled themselves on other rows. I duly followed suit, resting my head on my squashed up handbag, and we all fell asleep. It must have looked like a makeshift morgue.

At one thirty we opened up the room and welcomed in the children to start their lesson. The doctor dressed up in her white coat and hat and popped on her stethoscope, and the clinic outside the classroom was in progress. It was a unique visit, and I could not really see it happening in Edinburgh somehow!

Tien Yen

18 January 2002

Today I was in heaven in my beloved Binh Lieu. The sun shone and burnt up the morning mist and the huge mountains loomed up, making a frame for a perfect picture. Buffalo were ploughing, but as yet the fields are dry and dusty. It is so hard to imagine that in a few months every shade of green will be parading along the roads and up the hillsides.

We met Mrs Mai and Mr Sun, the deputy headmaster, who told us that the schedule for the preschool classes had been changed; instead of the morning lessons we had anticipated, the classes were now held in the afternoon. This is partly to do with the winter season, for it is very cold in the morning, especially high in the mountains. The children usually have more than an hour's walk before they get to school, which starts officially at seven thirty in the morning, so it is a little more humane to hold the class when the sun is higher in the sky and the rooms are warmer.

We had some time on our hands so we decided to visit the market at the foothills of the mountains, about three kilometres from the Chinese border. I was entranced, as always, with the aristocratic Dau women with their tall red boxes on their shaved heads, clustered in groups all red and black and exotically embroidered. They were very shy about being photographed but one woman did come forward and wanted to be snapped with her husband. He was in green army fatigues and wore a green pith helmet. They were an attractive couple, almost Edwardian in their formality, and had such serious faces. With their matching gold teeth they smiled just as I clicked, and I shall get a copy to give them. I can imagine it on their 'mantelpiece' where it will be a record of their early days as a married couple, before they become worn down from their hard lives and many children.

As we visited we heard many stories of tragedies that befall so many children, their lives lost through carelessness, accident and disease. The new incentive is to limit the number of children to two in each family, which is perhaps more manageable than the ten to twelve that was normal two generations ago. We were told of one grandmother in a village who had twelve children but gave seven away. She wasn't sure how many grandchildren she had, and she didn't really care; she just bothered with the ones who visited her. Life seems so cheap when you hear of it described so matter-of-factly.

After the Dau couple moved away, Mr Trinh felt it was time for lunch but, as there was nothing on offer at ten thirty in the morning, he decided to do it himself. He just made himself at home in a shack of a local restaurant, and when I came back later after cruising around and buying a scrubbing brush, I found a puddle of blood at the back of the corrugated iron lean-to, and there was the maestro plucking his chickens. We companionably sucked the sweet juice out of great sticks of sugar cane then spat out the dried-out fibres as the chickens boiled. Then, at about eleven –thirty, we ate salad leaves dipped in fish sauce, home-made rice noodles and a platter of artistically arranged chicken pieces, including feet and heart.

After lunch we set off on our mission to climb the mountains up to where the schools are nestled. I have never seen such stunning scenery. There were soaring peaks atop rugged mountains, sweeping wintry rice terraces that could have housed a Greek amphitheatre, huge clumps of bamboo and pine forests. We walked through a spice forest of cinnamon and star aniseed, and the smell was overpowering. Mo and I broke off a branch and nibbled the bark as we climbed, savouring the hot spice burning our tongues.

The Dau children we met were lovely. All of them wore red scarves on their heads, as they don't shave them until they are about twelve years old. They were open mouthed when they saw me, their first foreigner ever, and were intrigued by my blonde hair. I suppose it was a plus that I was wearing a safety pin on my shirt, given to me by a Dau woman in the market. They normally wear six to ten at a time for good luck (as well as to hold their shirts together). Mine did the trick, and I was made welcome.

The schools were made out of mud squashed into latticework, covered by a tin roof. There were lots of holes where the mud had fallen out, but the girls had made the best of what they had and had stuck pictures up to make the rooms more attractive. I just wonder what happens when it rains... There were no tables; everything takes place on a mat, but that is all right. Songs are sung, numbers and words are learned and a more child-friendly atmosphere is slowly replacing the rigid formality of rote learning.

The teachers were pleased to see me and want me to stay overnight the next time. I know how they feel, and can recognise their isolation and loneliness. It reminded me of the quote from Shakespeare's *Richard II* about feeling vulnerable and human, no matter whom you are:

> *Throw away respect,*
> *Tradition, form and ceremonious duty*
> *For you have but mistook me all this while*
> *I live with bread like you, feel want*
> *Taste grief, need friends.*

I am glad I made the effort to climb the mountain and take the time to visit and encourage these girls in one of the most isolated teaching posts in the country, where they get such paltry praise or value. Their education office only pays them VND 80,000 a month, which is around £4.

I fear they will leave unless they get a better incentive, for even the teachers in Tien Yen and Ba Chi receive VND 200,000. I asked Mrs Mai on their behalf if something could be done, but she more or less said, 'What do they need money for, living up in the mountains?'

When we got back to the car, Mr Trinh was very relaxed after his afternoon siesta. He took us to Mr Sun's house to get some special Binh Lieu honey, stored in Hanoi Beer bottles. I stupidly went to the loo in Mr Sun's house, a very dark affair around the back. I fumbled for the 'room' and couldn't find any shiny white porcelain, so went and asked Mrs Mai. She pointed to a drain that went out of the wall and told me to get on with it. When I finished she charged in with a basin of water and whooshed the floor, and everything went the way of all things.

I wonder what happens if you have a seriously upset tummy, or the person before you has? I pondered all this on the way back, as the sun dipped low in the sky and turned everything pure gold.

Tien Yen
27 January 2002

Days are running into one another, and small changes have been made to make my life easier. I moved out of the office and have a room in Bac Mai's guesthouse up the street from the SCF house. Xuan calls it Gael's Kingdom, as it perches high above the road. I sit out on my balcony and can look over the town towards the mountains in the distance, as well as viewing all the street dramas below me. It is a small room, but it has its own toilet and shower, so I feel I have a little privacy at the end of the day, a chance to separate from work and a place to read or write letters.

Last week we went down to Hanoi to attend the Education Forum, which fell on the wettest day of the year. We sat at tables covered in super white tablecloths. From the knee down most people were soaked, their trouser legs two-toned, owing to the universal form of transport being the motorbike.

I have been assigned a new translator, called Thau. She is quiet, petite and friendly. She looks so fragile and gets very carsick, so I am concerned about her ability to last through the journeys to the schools.

We have had another few days of training, this time on Life Skills, run by two very experienced ladies from the Ministry of Education and Training. They enjoyed their stay with us in Tien Yen and even joined in the impromptu dance lessons that Hiep conducts whenever we have a few minutes to spare. He has been giving us extra tuition with our dance classes in the Post Office, giving us lots of practise with the cha-cha and the rumba.

These last few days the office has been quiet; the training is over and the car has gone back to Hanoi, leaving only

Thau and me here. We sit in the evenings, and it is very domestic. Hang and Thau have been helping me to pin and tack the silk on to the hexagon shapes, and I stitch up the flowers. The CD of Westlife plays 'My Love' over and over, as well as 'Solida' which is Thau's favourite. The days are cold and misty and I paint pictures for teachers' classrooms and Thau helps me translate key words.

I have been taking Mr Darcy for long walks, and on the way back from one of these we met Minh who invited us in to look at her new room. It is beautiful, all tiled blue with huge palms and ferns in pots and there is a big mirror on the wall. Mr Darcy disgraced himself as he peed in a corner... I was black affronted.

Tien Yen
31 January 2002

We went to Binh Lieu again, and this time it was a Macbeth soup bowl of mist and fog, with red slimy roads. The mountains rose like a pen and ink sketch, all blurred and out of focus, as though too much water had made the edges run. A buffalo had been slaughtered and huge red chunks of meat filled a basket lined with banana leaves at the side of the road.

The first school was a nightmare. The poor girl had little control of her class, and older kids harassed her through the open window. They sometimes jumped in and pulled pictures off the wall or even threw stones at her. She only earns VND 60,000 a month; a mere £3. She told us that her mother is paralysed, her father loves another woman and her sister has to stay home from school to take care of her mother. She looked so sad, and she is only nineteen. We promised to try and speak to her headmaster to see if he could enforce some discipline.

The road to the next school was cut into the edge of a hillside, and the slimy red soil was held together by loose boulders. Sometimes, as we veered towards the edge, I just shut my eyes tight as the drop would have been fatal. Great swirls of fog made visibility almost non-existent.

We made it, however, and while the journey may have been treacherous, the school was wonderful. The teacher, Nhan, had brought in young trees in pots and the children were busy matching them to pictures of the fruit and identifying the vocabulary. They played games then acted out a story. They seemed so happy and their Vietnamese was good. Nhan was looking very smart in a green trouser suit. She kept holding my hand and told me that I had kissed her daughter at the last training. As she was about forty-five to fifty, I was wondering whom on earth I had kissed!

Then she told us her story. She came from just outside of Hanoi and had been a soldier in the American War. She and her soldier fiancé had planned to be married, but only ten days before their wedding he had been shot. For twenty-seven years she had lived with her mother, until last year when she met and married the chief of this village in the northern district of Binh Lieu, about one mile from China; they now have a six-month-old baby girl (whom I do remember kissing). This amazing lady had the most sticking-out teeth in the deepest shade of brown I have ever seen. It's good to know that love is blind.

Thau fell into the river on the way back and had to splodge to the car in her very high platform trainers... not very elegant.

And it rains and rains. We sit in jackets and scarves. Silent days.

Hanoi
10 February 2002

Chuc Mung Nam Moi (Happy New Year). It is the eve of *Tet*, or Chinese New Year, and the whole of Hanoi is shopping. Red boxes of biscuits, red paper lanterns, tinsel, brandy, cellophane-wrapped gift baskets, fruit and flowers are all on everyone's list, and there is even more colour than usual and an electric feeling of celebration in the air.

I remember when I first came here the traffic terrified me; I was appalled by the lawlessness and the complete lack of concern shown by people as they cross streets. I did eventually join the throng by climbing onto a *xe om*, clutching the driver and spending the trip tense and with my eyes shut tight. Today I was as calm and relaxed as though on a garden swing. I noticed other passengers, a lot of them small children and sometimes the full family complement. All had this 'other world peacefulness' on their faces as we weaved through thick spaghetti messes of taxis, buses, ladies carrying poles with vegetables balanced in their baskets and about a million jay walkers. I just sat and felt quite ethereal.

I was still floating from my visit the previous evening to the Hanoi Opera House – beautiful, imposing and presenting an image of another era. It is a direct copy of the one in Paris, though about half the size, but I don't believe there is a phantom haunting the back stage.

I listened to the National Orchestra Strings section play selections from Elgar, Tchaikovsky and Rostokovich, then made my way back to my hotel and woke up with big plans to visit the West Lake and see the riot of colour in Nghi Tam Street.

For the Vietnamese this is the equivalent of going to

choose a Christmas tree, and I found both sides of the road decked out like mini forests of peach blossom and kumquat trees. In between there were orchids, poinsettias, chrysanthemums, hyacinths and tulips. Sellers sit like brothel madams, waiting for the vehicles to pull up and select and bargain for the sweetest flower. There was a constant stream of kerb-crawlers.

As the traffic drives off, I am reminded of Birnam Wood in Shakespeare's *Macbeth* as the flowering forest moves around, strapped on to the back of the motorbikes, through the streets of the city.

My head and eyes were full of flowers, so when I saw a sign advertising foot massages, and feeling like I'd just walked for about two million miles, I realised I was tired and decided to have a go. It was heavenly, not only for my feet but also my back, head and shoulders. My young man had hands that were like steel and yet as gentle as a lover... I spent an hour being pummelled and prodded and caressed. I walked out feeling as though I was walking on a cushion of air and sat down almost immediately as I saw some ladies crowded round a food stall on the pavement. They asked me to join them and, as the 'inner woman' now needed some attention, I was quite tempted by what I thought was fish and chips. The chief cook sat in pyjamas and squatted as she watched her pots bubbling with boiling oil.

She had a flour batter mixture and when I got my portion, wrapped up in a piece of newspaper, it turned out to be banana fritters and chips, all squashed together in a very bright yellow mess. It was very tasty and the company was friendly, all discussing the price of peach trees for *Tet*. I decided to really go overboard and had another portion; they threw in a cup of tea as well, and I paid my VND 2,000 and walked off feeling very content. Beautiful music, stunning flowers, a pampered body and a full tummy... could this be happiness?

Hanoi

15 February 2002

It cost me a grand total of a million dong (about £50) to fly to Son La in a dinky toy aeroplane to spend the three days of the *Tet* holiday with Xuan and her lovely family. Son La is a town that is en route to Dien Bien Phu, the site of the great Ho Chi Minh victory against the French in 1954. It is a paradise of limestone mountains, similar to those that rise out of the sea in Halong Bay, and is home to the Thai ethnic minority people. I found them the most gentle, beautiful and dignified of all the groups I have met so far. These are quite a different ethnic minority group, and not related at all to the people of Thailand. The Thai are split into two groups – the Black Thai and the White Thai. They have lived in northwest Vietnam since ancient times, and have their own language and their own Sanskrit-style writing system.

Tet was like Christmas and New Year all rolled into one. Peach blossom decorated with tinsel and balloons featured in every house; food preparation was a top priority and flowers were arranged in all the rooms. The Abba hit 'Happy New Year' blared from every outlet from Hanoi to the mountains. It was incredible.

I was made so welcome by Xuan and her family, and did all the things that were expected of me. I drank rice wine through bamboo straws and prayed twice a day at the family altar. I slept on a thin bamboo mattress alongside Xuan, her mother and her niece, and awoke in the mornings wondering where on earth I was and whose face was lying next to mine; the comings and goings during the night meant that I would often wake up next to a different person from the one I had gone to sleep beside.

Like a Scottish New Year, where people go 'first footing'

or visiting neighbours, Tet honoured the same tradition. We visited so many of Xuan's family and friends, eating festive foods and drinking wine in each house.

We went in a convoy of motorbikes to visit a Thai village miles off the beaten track in the mountains. There we were welcomed into a bamboo house on stilts, where the large upper floor comprised living, sleeping and cooking areas. This space was shared by about three couples, with only a thin curtain dividing each one's privacy. It reminded me of a boarding school dormitory. We got blitzed on rice wine and ate some very unusual food; Xuan whispered to me, 'Just don't ask, Gael!' To this day I'm not sure exactly what I did eat. I ended up playing a game with all the children that involved pinging a sort of small round disc off our thighs into a bull's eye about ten metres away.

We said goodbye to our hosts, and as we zoomed off on the motorbikes I was a bit alarmed when my driver, who was very flushed, told me how much she enjoys riding her motorbike very fast as it makes her heart jump up and down! When we arrived at the next house, much to the bemusement of our new hosts, we all just lay down on the floor in a drunken heap and had a short siesta. Needless to say there was more rice wine waiting when we woke up.

The next day Xuan and I visited the sights around Son La, and I read that it was once the site of a French penal colony in which anti-colonial revolutionaries were incarcerated. The old French Prison has been partially restored in the interests of historical tourism. Rebuilt turrets and watchtowers stand guard over the remains of cells, inner walls and a famous lone surviving peach tree. The tree, which blooms with traditional *Tet* flowers, was planted in the compound by To Hieu, a former inmate from the 1940s. To Hieu has subsequently been immortalised, with various landmarks about the town named after him.

We then relaxed in the hot springs in our own private, fully tiled bathtub. We floated for an hour in the hot water and hoped that its mythical qualities would enhance and rejuvenate our skin. I'm not sure if they did, but for a while it seemed that our eyes shone brighter and all my laugh lines had smoothed out.

All of these visits were embroidered with tales and customs of Xuan's childhood during the difficult 1980s, when the communists had the country by the throat and families lived with only the most dismal ration coupons. Poverty was dire. It is so hard to imagine now, with the colourful produce overflowing in the markets, that just a few years ago there was no such thing.

It was strange to come back to Hanoi and find the streets empty and all the shops shut. It felt like a ghost town. I met up with Richard and we went to a party and had a wonderful time, singing melancholy Scottish songs about dark islands and the cares of tomorrow, and the next morning I woke up with a sore head.

It was Valentine's Day and Richard brought me a red rose and coffee, and somehow the day passed in a haze of watching movies and walking by the lake. It had been raining so there was a mist and the lake looked like a slightly blurred water painting. As night fell the city lights were muted in the drizzle. We didn't want to drink in the bars so we bought a fish, flapping madly in its plastic carrier bag, and took it back to the house where we cooked it, drank wine, and moved the red rose down to the table to join the candle light.

After wandering around the West Lake the next morning and visiting the pagoda, we decided to hire a motorbike and get out of the city for a while. We headed for the pottery villages that line the Red River and, after buying a couple of souvenirs, we found some reject blue and white pots piled up behind a wall. We took two, strapped them onto the back of the bike, and set off for the pagodas.

Because it was *Tet*, the monks invited us in and gave us tea and mandarins and sticky rice cake. It was quite awkward to accept so much hospitality with our limited Vietnamese but, if we couldn't talk, at least we could show our willingness to eat, so we did that.

We crossed the river on a tiny little ferry, with all of humanity squashed on board, and came to more pagodas on the other side. I was entranced with one that had just had all its paintwork redone, so we went in to admire all the beautiful murals depicting dragons and flowers and birds. We realised that there was a whole group of old-age pensioners sitting on the floor at the foot of the Buddha, so we turned to leave, but they were very insistent that we should join them. They gave us tea, and smiled... their faces were gentle, their eyes creased with a million wrinkles and their teeth stained black. They handed us a plate of betel nut and motioned to us to chew.

I knew there was lots of folklore attached to the betel nut and the chewing of it. That, as well as coating the teeth with lacquer, tattooing, and living in stilt houses, belongs to an Asian culture that predates all Chinese and Hindu influence. The chewing of the betel still continues today, especially in the countryside and amongst women, and a plate with the leaf, the nut and the lime are offered as one offers a cigarette in the West. It is the starter for conversation, and it is seen as a symbol of love and marriage. It is the symbol of a union that lasts until death.

There is a story of a girl who mistook her husband's brother for her husband. This resulted in the death of the young man, who was overcome with guilt by the bank of a river and was then turned into a limestone rock. The husband went in search of his brother and was overcome with grief at the consequence of the genuine mistake. He too then died beside the river and the spirits turned him into an areca palm tree. The young wife, full of remorse, set off in search of her husband. She was overcome with hunger and tiredness and came upon the rock on which the palm tree was growing. The young woman embraced the trunk of the tree and she also died. The spirits then turned her into a climbing plant, the betel creeper. As a symbol of this story, the betel is served with lime and the trio are united for eternity.

Sitting on the floor of the temple, I chewed until suddenly my face grew hot and I spat out the red juice into a can full of other discarded spittle. I was gagging and fighting the urge to be sick. Richard just laughed, but the ladies were very proud of my efforts and were grinning and congratulating me.

When we got back to Hanoi later that evening we were walking through the streets to go to a restaurant for something to eat when Richard said something silly and insensitive about our blue and white pots, and I just could not stop crying. I felt so vulnerable and had the weird sensation of floating a little above my body. The betel may have a lot of history, but nobody told me that it was a hallucinogenic drug!

The world has returned to normal; the city has filled up once again with all the motorbikes and people have come back from visiting relatives in other parts of the country. The noise and chaos has resumed, but the sun is shining and it's hot. Bich rang to say hello. She has had a wonderful time, flying up and down to Ho Chi Minh City and visiting relatives in the countryside. I asked politely after her family. All is well apart from her husband, who has been ill. In true Vietnamese fashion, she put that down to the change in the wind. I had my doubts, for I had already spotted the three bottles of Johnny Walker Black Label that she bought in Bangkok! Anyway, I thought a change in the wind only brought Mary Poppins.

Yesterday I was feeling melancholy. To add to that I have

had my hair shorn like Samson, so I am feeling very sensitive and Richard is out of town.

I have to go to Hue next Monday for a conference. Perhaps then life will return to normal, when we get back to Tien Yen for school visits, the quilt and Mr Darcy!

Tien Yen

4 March 2002

It has been a week now since we made the twelve-hour journey from Hanoi to Hue on the overnight sleeper. The whole staff of SCF (UK) in Vietnam were off to their annual conference, so there was a lot of chattering as compartments were changed and everyone found friends that they wanted to share with.

There were four in a compartment and it really was quite comfortable, with a toilet, shower and bunks with fresh linen. I shared with Anne and Bich and her mother, but I didn't sleep for ages. Instead I watched the almost full moon stay constant in a clear sky as the landscape rushed by in dark silhouettes. I was unsettled because I had spent the afternoon with Richard. We had walked around the lake in Lenin Park, then sat on a stone bench under a weeping willow and talked about our early childhood. Images from another time had arisen, and I knew then that I wanted to recapture those elusive moments; words were chasing themselves around my brain and I couldn't sleep.

We arrived in Hue at dawn and I was so glad that I had left my fleece and possum socks behind, as being so much further south the temperature was sticky and hot.

The first afternoon I walked for miles before succumbing to the charms of a cyclo driver who took me on a small tour. I saw and smelt the market; by four o'clock everything was turning into a mushy compost, and I saw my first victims of war, men with no legs and begging bowls. So little sympathy, and only passing charity as a reward for being alive, compared to the glorious monuments that mark those who died.

My driver took me to the Thien Mu Pagoda just as the

sun set. A huge orange globe hung over the Perfume River, making all the trees stand black and form a frame around the beautiful tower. The sky was full of dragonflies, and white-robed monks ate dinner whilst young, shaven-headed, brown-robed novices sprang about doing kung fu exercises. I stood and looked and prayed. It was so quiet and I felt so serene. I wandered back to the steps and saw the peaceful river and the sampans; it was hard to imagine that this was the scene of such horrific bombing and warfare.

Stupidly I had left my camera in the hotel, so instead I just kept blinking my eyes to record all the day-to-day life that gets enacted on the street or through the open doors of the houses. I saw a man clipping his toenails in a restaurant, his feet up on the table. A lady wearing a beautiful blue *ao dai* was praying at the altar by the front door of her house, her hands clasping smouldering incense sticks. A pretty girl with glossy hair the colour of ebony was making an orange cat stretch up on its tippy toes.

We passed a Carmelite convent that is home to '*les babas avec no mamas or papas*', according to my guide. He rubbed his fingers and thumbs together to suggest money and the possibility of me buying one. US$ 20,000 is the current asking price, and most babies go to Germany, Canada and the USA. France used to be the highest taker, with thousands going every year, but last year new regulations meant that only twelve went. In 1995, 1,400 babies went to the French with a sixty million US dollar income generated from baby sales.

As the sky darkened I found the moon to be a perfect circle. It was the first full moon of the Lunar New Year – very significant – and it was so low in the sky it seemed to be balancing in the branches of a flame tree growing beside the walls that enclose the historic citadel.

Man and nature have been cruel to Hue. Because the mountains are so close to the sea the area has the highest rainfall in Vietnam. Everything rots in the soggy climate and plants take root in the brickwork, eventually bringing the beautiful, historic buildings down.

During the *Tet* Offensive of 1968, Hue suffered some of the bloodiest fighting and cruellest retribution of any town during the Vietnam War. After the North Vietnamese Army had taken over the city, they took revenge on the population by removing 'uncooperative' elements. The army victimised about three thousand civilians, including Buddhist monks, priests, intellectuals, and anyone considered remotely sympathetic to the southern regime. Their grim fate was either execution by firing squad, decapitation or being buried alive. Although I looked, I saw nothing about this in Hue's War Museum.

Over one hundred temples and historic sites have been lost forever, destroyed by war. However, enough of old Hue remains to recall its former glory as the official capital for a hundred and forty-three years, located in the geographic centre of Vietnam.

For all the problems of the past, much rebuilding and restoration has been carried out. The Forbidden City, which was originally constructed in 1804 (a copy of the one in Beijing), has now been returned to its former glory. Some work has smacks of communist kitsch and one wonders if the improvements are for the better. Like all renovation, I suppose there are arguments for both sides.

Our guide was a hoot at one Royal Tomb as he pointed out the new mosaic work depicting different creatures, and described the phoenix as the 'harbinger of peace'. I think he had swallowed a dictionary, but it was reassuring to know that Hue had followed the phoenix's mythological example and had indeed risen from the ashes.

The following day was taken up with presentations, but, as the sun went down, I set off with Xuan and her friends on the back of a motorbike and we zoomed about the city in convoy. We ate all the local specialities, and I just loved the grilled spring roll kebabs that we had to roll ourselves in rice paper, adding lettuce and cucumber, then dipping them into a peanut sauce. *Ngon lam!* We drove down to the riverside and drank strange sweetcorn tea and then went to get measured for our *ao dais*.

The SCF Conference itself combined both offices of Hanoi and Ho Chi Minh City, and presentations included all the projects that Save the Children support in Vietnam. I heard about child trafficking, social protection, HIV/AIDS, credit and finance, education, relief and emergency aid. Everyone was very proud of his or her own corner and, of course, a special item on the agenda was the imminent visit of Princess Anne.

After the Conference we got a chance to go on tours, and now I am truly pagoda'd and tombed out – such grandeur, opulence and ornate decoration in a country that has seen such dire poverty! One king was very keen on philosophy and sat by his lotus pond where he composed four thousand poems. He had a hundred and four wives but no children, and he was seriously depressed, so he prepared his mausoleum sixteen years before his death. He chose the most beautiful and peaceful site, surrounded by Scots pines, so I hope he is finding happiness in the hereafter.

Later we all dressed up for dinner and a sail in a wonderful dragon boat on the Perfume River. We all wore our new *ao dais*; Xuan in white was very traditional, whereas mine was black, sleeveless with a low neck. I had images of Catherine Deneuve in Indochine, so I felt *très elegante*!

During the cruise we were all given clothes in which to 'dress up', as we were to re-enact the days of the Royal Court. Naturally, Bill, our dashing director, was elected the King, and we were all his mandarins and concubines. The costumes made us as colourful and flamboyant as peacocks and parrots.

The moon was still huge and hung like a giant round lantern in the sky, mirroring our little human attempts at giving light as we lit candles, placed them in cardboard containers and set them off to sail away into the darkness. We were supposed to make a wish and I suppose we did, but our colourful floating palace drifted away and left the tiny collection of human hopes and dreams to splutter and die in the black river.

I met Jo, the Medical Officer for Asia and the Pacific, who specialises in HIV/AIDS. I had to smile as we had a serious conversation whilst he was dressed in an emerald green robe with an amazing headdress trimmed with pompoms and sparklers. Being from India, he was quite a regal spectacle. I was in brilliant yellow satin with a neat little yellow hat, the costume of a concubine I think! He told me about his work in Calcutta and I was fascinated. He and his wife lived in the Red Light district as part of a medical/education project, teaching literacy and giving support to the sex workers in the brothels. Over a period of three years, they helped the women to form a union in order to empower themselves, and now, as a result of this work, the women have control of a one million US dollar budget for education, protection and healthcare.

He told me that the literacy programme was a little more specific than learning by ABC, for the idea was to gather job-specific vocabulary and make primer reading books using these words. They were relevant to the women's experience and could literally expand from what the women knew, thus extending their knowledge. Booklets were written entitled My First Customer, What I Felt Like After Three Joints, and so forth. Key words were then taken and learnt, so the reading was 'look-say' as well as phonetic. Not that different from what I do in Primary 1, though the slang of sex and drugs is usually learnt behind the bike sheds.

Jo was interested in my work in Tien Yen and the

controversial issue of giving a Vietnamese curriculum to the ethnic minority groups. But with the modernisation that is occurring in Vietnam and the media expanding to even the remotest places, it is inevitable that people will need the tools to keep abreast of these changes; I feel they deserve the chance, at least, to make their own choices. I suppose it is the same everywhere, for if the young people go to the cities, who will plant the rice and take care of the buffalo? I witnessed the same thing in Portree on the Isle of Skye, where the young people were no longer interested in staying to raise sheep and work the crofts that were a way of life that had existed for centuries. The opportunities gained with Certificates of Higher Education meant that young people were lured to the big cities of London, Glasgow and Edinburgh.

By Friday our group had fragmented; some had left and some had other workshops, so I teamed up with the group from Ho Chi Minh City and we went to the Love Pagoda, which sits on an island only reached by a boat trip on a sampan. It was so idyllic and peaceful. After looking around, we got the chance to do the Fortune Sticks. We had to kneel down, whisper our name and date of birth to Buddha, and then shake the canister with the sticks until one fell out. The number on the stick was matched to the appropriate fortune and we held it tightly in our hands, for we had to hide it and read it on the boat. A group of police and government officials had arrived and were drinking tea in an adjoining room; apparently it is just not on to have all this jiggery pokery going on in the temple.

On the boat and on the bus we all compared notes. The fortunes don't mince words, and some are quite ruthless. I noticed one girl particularly downcast at her gloomy prediction, as I think she was hoping for a reconciliation with her husband who had abandoned her and her little boy. Mine told me that I am supposed to do well in examinations or a new job, but love would be difficult owing to distance and separation. Maybe I should take up cards... I might have more luck with the King of Hearts in the pack, as I certainly don't seem to have much luck in the real world!

In the afternoon I revisited the market and got lost in all the stalls and produce, ending up beside the strangest combination. One side displayed fruit and vegetables and on the other were about twelve hairdressing shacks, all in a row. I had to laugh as the overwhelming smell was 'Head and Shoulders', and women in curlers sat in the doorways whilst others lay with their heads covered in frothy suds. One was having her facial hair removed whilst her fingers were soaking in soapy water in little fish sauce bowls. It was all so intimate and yet so public, as I made my way round pyramids of mangoes, baskets of live chickens and great trays of pearl-coloured rice.

I am now back in Tien Yen, and I had forgotten what a nice town it is and how fond I have become of so many of my neighbours, but the terrible thing is that Mr Darcy was stolen the night before we got back. We know his fate and we knew it was a risk, but now that this has happened I cannot describe how sad it is. We believe he was stolen by heroin addicts who needed the money, and the dog meat restaurant would have paid about VND 400,000; around £20. We know our friends on the street would never have hurt him. I feel so bad because, for the last month, Hang had practically ignored him; he was either chained up or abandoned to run free, and he would have missed all our comings and goings. He was so friendly and had no fear of anyone. Poor Darcy, he had so much love from us all and must have felt so betrayed. He was only seven months old.

Tien Yen

11 March 2002

Xuan has been crying all week. I am just stunned and upset, and keep hoping that Mr Darcy will come bouncing in. Hang is quiet for she knows that Xuan is angry with her for being so careless, and Trinh just laughs at all this sentimentality.

We have had a week of visitors, including Bich, and Claire, a French consultant who has been working on an Early Childhood programme with SCF (France). The house is in chaos with meetings and planning and reviewing going on all the time. I have been trying to keep my mind off Mr Darcy's fate by keeping busy and visiting schools along with the other team, so my teachers have all been pleased to have the unexpected visits. It has been lovely having Claire to talk to; I had forgotten what it was like to have someone to chat to during dinner, as normally I sit silently and eat and listen to all the chattering going on around me. I didn't realise how lonely and withdrawn I had become. I sat with Claire on my balcony and we drank beer and compared jobs and lives and experiences; the street was quiet and it was peaceful sitting like two eagles overlooking the town.

Now everyone has gone, and as I write I am sitting in a T-shirt and suddenly notice that it is warm, and the sun has some heat at last. Perhaps winter has gone. I am listening to the loud music from across the street and, as it is only eight o'clock in the morning, I wonder at the total lack of consideration there is for anyone else; why does the whole town have to listen to the music of Westlife just because one woman does? Why does a vehicle have to peep its horn at five o'clock when everyone is still asleep and the town is still dark? Why is there a need for the constant peeping of horns anyway? I listen to the noise, the engines, the killing of screaming pigs, the total disregard for anyone else's feelings and despair for these people who cannot tolerate silence or being alone.

I am so out of sorts. Since they killed our dog, I am now seeing all the Vietnamese faults, whereas before I used to try and disguise them and see everyone through rose-tinted glasses. Now I see everything: the inability to queue, the need to be first (even overtaking on a hill with a blind corner), the elbows jarring as they shove you out of the way so that they can do everything before you, ramming their passport and tickets on top of yours. It is just unbelievable. The casual peeling of fruit and throwing and spitting all the skin and pips on to the floor, the tossing of chicken bones and meat gristle under the table, and the disgusting state of some restaurants. I am sickened by the coughing, snorting, spitting, the continual aggressive 'Hello, what is your name?' and the vile smell of pee along the pavements owing to men and kids urinating everywhere. Ooooo grrrr... though I know it will pass and I shall regain my equilibrium. Each culture has its irritations, I know, and I am not so shallow as to think that my home country is so perfect and its values are relevant in this one. But they are my values, and how much more of this country's values I can take, I cannot tell.

Thau and I got hopelessly lost in the forest on Wednesday. We had walked the one and a half hours to a school, had seen the teacher and had stayed and helped her with a language lesson. Then we set off back to the car and had to walk as though on a tight rope, balancing on an irrigation dyke in the middle of a rice field. I couldn't help noticing the water on each side held great black clouds of jellied tadpoles. We were overpowered by the smell of grapefruit blossoms everywhere, a rich, cloying, sickly sweet smell, as the flowers hung in dense white clusters all around us.

I remember Xuan telling me that one of the teachers had asked a class why they needed irrigation dykes for the paddy fields, and a child had answered that they were built so that people could join together and work together and so be united for the common good. Uncle Ho's teaching still reaches even the mountainous regions!

I was gazing about at the beautiful white poinsettias growing wild and free, intermingled with jungle creepers, and became intrigued by the whispery delicate fungi growing on the buffalo poo. Suddenly I realised that we were lost. We had missed the turn-off, and as the sky darkened, a fine drizzle soon turned to heavy drops of rain. We walked and walked through the forest like Hansel and Gretel, seeing no landmarks that we could recognise, but it grew colder and our feeling of alarm grew as we knew the car was supposed to collect us at twelve o'clock. We passed the odd hunter carrying great knives, but as they only spoke their ethnic language they couldn't respond to Thau's questions as to which way we should go. They must have been surprised seeing us so out of our way.

We did come across the odd cluster of mud houses, villages in the middle of nowhere, and unexpectedly met a pretty girl whom I knew from the health visits of the previous week. She had told us how her husband had delivered both her children, cut the cord and bathed the baby, so unlike the stories of the men in the cities, who adopt quite a different attitude. They concentrate more on celebrating with their friends, drinking rice wine or beer, than giving their wife support through labour. Mostly it is a macho, bravado sort of thing – a result of being the pampered male child and favourite of the mother. Men seem at a loss to know how to be emotionally supportive to their wives. After her last baby, this Dau girl had had an

IUD fitted, but it was inserted too soon after the birth, before the uterus had returned to its normal size, and so she was in a lot of pain. Birth control is given free after two children, but any aftercare costs have to be met by the woman herself. Treatment and removal of the device was more than she could afford, so both she and her husband had developed an infection. Luckily Bich gave her some money and her problem was treated.

There are many women who suffer gynaecological problems from working all day submerged in water. It is reassuring to know that there is a heightened awareness of these problems and health clinics offering check-ups are now being set up. It is still early days but it is a start, so hopefully infections and diseases will be picked up and treated.

Girls generally marry young and go to live with the husband's family. This is quite normal, but in one village we were told about a girl who was so unhappy after she had had a row with her husband that she had gone into the forest and eaten some deadly leaves, thus committing suicide. So much despair and unhappiness was caused, yet the father-in-law pointed to where she was buried as though he was referring to a pig or a dog. The young bride was only eighteen.

Thau and I discussed all this as we continued on our path, the rain now heavier and the forest darker. We searched for familiar landmarks and wondered if anyone would come looking for us; a gingerbread house would have been very welcome at that time.

We were saved by some schoolchildren who were sheltering under a tree, playing cards. Their Vietnamese was about as good as mine, but Thau was able to understand and get the general directions for the road. Off we sloshed through the mud, praying we wouldn't slip, and, after what felt like Napoleon's retreat from Moscow, we saw the road.

When we got back to Tien Yen, I was just so glad to see the white rice, emerald green spinach and pieces of deep-fried squid for lunch. It is amazing how hungry you become when you are lost, and my longing for the little home comforts was overwhelming. I used to empathise so much with Bilbo Baggins in Tolkien's *The Hobbit*. Poor Bilbo Baggins would end up on some adventure to rid the world of evil, and all he really wanted was to sit by his fireside and hear the kettle start to whistle its familiar signal for a nice cup of tea. I hated *The Lord of the Rings* as the adventure was too long and too frightening, and the references to 'home' were so remote. I just wanted the little hobbits to get back and sit down by their fireside.

I was very comforted to be back, lying on my bed, reading my book, feeling safe for a little while as the rain continued to drum down and fall in great waterfalls off the roof and the afternoon grew dark.

Because the winter was over, our visits to the schools in Binh Lieu were now scheduled for the morning, and we realised we would have to make an early start in order to climb the mountain. It made sense to stay the night in Binh Lieu and be ready to leave with the dawn.

Xuan, Thau, Mr Trinh and I loaded up the car with the clothes that we had bought in Mon Cai with money donated by the British Embassy in Hanoi. Thau and I had had a very successful shopping trip and had bought over a hundred tracksuits to be given to all the children in the preschool classes. When asked how best to use the monies available, we felt that the lack of suitable clothing was of top priority. The winters were freezing and the children we had seen were often in rags, with bare legs and cotton shirts that invariably had no buttons.

We arrived in Binh Lieu in the evening and checked into a very imposing hotel, directly opposite the pink palace of the People's Committee. The hotel was very communist, sparse and cheap, with most of the fittings broken. The towels they gave us were the size of face cloths and already wet, so I went out and bought a new one, the only choice being a small hand towel, so I had to settle for that.

Mrs Mai took us to dinner at a very modest restaurant, where the family was all watching a Korean 'noodle' film. When we asked for something to eat, there was a definite feeling that they were doing us a great favour. The mother dragged herself up from the film and started to gather some greenery together. I had to look away as a brown chicken stalked up and down on the work surface... at least I knew the main course was fresh.

We drank some wine and beer and toasted each other's health, then after about forty minutes a wonderful meal of boiled chicken pieces arrived, followed by a thick soup with cellophane noodles, chives and coriander. It was delicious.

Next morning at about half past six we had breakfast in a hovel at the back of the market. Wood stoves held black ingrained pans, boiling and bubbling like Macbeth's cauldrons. This was obviously the kitchen, placed strategically at the doorway, and we were shown to a table with a greasy red cloth. It had a panoramic view of all the kids peeing in the dirt outside. I removed a syringe from my seat, prompting gales of laughter from the cook who explained that she had a medical problem, not for drugs, ha ha ha ... Oh God.

We all had special Binh Lieu noodles, this being the only dish on the menu. These were huge rice pancakes, steamed over the blackened stove and cut into strips with a big hunting knife, then rolled up and dipped into bowls with soy sauce and garlic. I picked one up and it felt like a limp penis. Mrs Mai ate about seven; I think I forced two.

A policeman came marching into the hovel and demanded my papers. No tourists are allowed in this area, owing to the sensitivity of the border crossing with China. I could not understand why this one region is so prickly about their nearest neighbour, but I presume it is a land issue. When the Chinese retreated in 1979, they still felt they had some rights to the land in Binh Lieu district. I am not sure what the police thought I was going to do about it, but Mrs Mai managed to reassure this officer that my mission was only connected with educational matters, so we were allowed to proceed.

We left and started the climb, up up up into the cloud-covered mountains. Once again we passed through the cinnamon forest but, it being spring now, we were able to enjoy the wild strawberries and the sweetness was wonderful after the stodgy noodles. The rest of the morning we spent on our knees on the cement floors of the classrooms, dressing the children in their new clothes. They were very suspicious at first; some would not try on the sweatshirt and instead sat and held it tightly in their laps. Dau girls wear silver torques around their necks, and headscarves, as it is not until puberty that they have to shave their heads. The mums and grannies crowded around the door and windows, and I noticed that they had watches and bunches of keys on their torques. Later one granny was so excited by a child's drawing that she came in waving her massive hunting knife about, obviously trying to describe how to draw some shape. The only way we could get her to leave was to point a camera at her… and then she ran.

The walk back down the hill was easier as the clothes had all been distributed. We were able to gaze about and I was struck again at the similarity of the mountain range and how much it reminded me of Scottish peaks at home. There was the gentle rise of the pine forests and the soft feel of the carpet of yellow needles underfoot. There was the familiar smell of pine resin and, ahead, the great shapes of the mountains. There was even some heather growing, white and bell-like, obviously some relation to the Scottish Erica.

I had a pang of longing for another time in my life and a white house in the northwest of Scotland that had been my home for so many years. I remember trying to describe it to Richard in Lenin Park in Hanoi as we tentatively exchanged small intimacies, and then later on the night train to Hue I attempted to piece together fragments of memories of Glenelg and my life with Dave and our three children. Happiness is something that you cannot hold on to or clasp tightly or achieve by endeavour. Some wise man said that sometimes we should pause in our pursuit of happiness and just be happy. Milton's words describe the complexities of such human contradictions much better than I ever could:

> *The mind is its own place and in itself*
> *Can make heaven of hell and hell of heaven.*

Perhaps it is all cyclic, like the moon, and happiness waxes and wanes. And we all have regrets for not taking advantage of a particular experience and enjoying it. I have a feeling that maybe Milton was right.

In retrospect I can see that events in life are so transient; today rapidly becomes no more than a memory, and ideally memories should be golden. I look at Richard and just love being with him. He makes me so happy but he doesn't feel the same and instead is in pursuit of his own elusive dream. But he has given my life here in Vietnam another dimension, and for that he will always be someone that I have felt love for. He gave me back my perspective and allowed me to remember things that I had wanted to forget.

That afternoon, as I stood in the pine forest in north Vietnam with the mists swirling around me, the years just fell away and I was thousands of miles across the sea in a completely different time dimension.

I remember when we saw it first, a solid white house, an old Free Church manse standing in a field of bracken, its windows boarded up. The floors sloped and gave way to the earth and the wind whistled down chimneys. Fires smoked through loose stonework where chimney linings had given way. The furniture was solid, brown, basic and mostly didn't match.

Its name was Creagan Mhor, which means 'Big Rock' in the Scottish Gaelic, and we saw it on a cold December afternoon, when the light had almost gone. Snow showers and hail fell on us as we walked through the fields to get to it, opening and closing three sets of gates. There was snow on the hills and the distant houses looked warm and welcoming, just smudges of yellow seen through closed curtains, scattered around the crofts.

We bought the house and lived there for the next eleven years.

It had been our dream and it embodied everything we had ever imagined. Standing alone, it looked to the hills and the sea. The Island of Eigg rose in the distance down the Sound of Sleat, and to the right was the south Skye peninsula. Behind were Mam Ratagan, Ben Capil and Ben Scrithail… all poetic mountain names conjuring up the bleakness of waterlogged marshy grazing lands, golden bracken and sunlight on the sea.

There were lazy days fishing for mackerel or casting into the deep, dark pools for trout and the elusive salmon, and later cleaning fish on the shore where gulls stalked and waited for the proffered head and guts. Wonderful smells of grilled fish and endless cups of tea, and coffees with neighbours.

I have two five-year diaries of those years. Reading them, the years become compressed and, as pages are flicked, the pain and worries of a child's sickness or earache whiz past. Somehow the actual hours are lost and only the milestone of the biro pen entry is there to trigger your memory of a neighbour's illness or death, disputes, the proud moment of a finished knitted masterpiece. Great and small achievements were all recorded faithfully as we watched the children grow and the house mend. April's entries, collecting primroses to make home-made wine... July, September, fishing, picnics, hill climbing, school concerts, Halloween parties and Christmas.

But Glenelg was beautiful, isolated and lonely. Dave was often working away for long periods of time, and I became involved with another man. How many times have I tried to analyse it, blamed A, B or C, gin, the weather or just human nature? Sometimes I feel that I am weeping inside when I think about it all. The heartbreaking sadness of the music. White, wintry showers and the scarlet berries of the rowan trees. Walking with the cruel wind whipping your face and the pure silence of the nights, black with the clearest, brightest stars.

I drove away from Glenelg to live in Edinburgh on 16 July 1994 and we sold the house in 1998, the same year that we divorced.

Misty mountains of Skye suddenly blurred and I heard the Vietnamese chatter of Thau and Mrs Mai; I realised that I was half a world away looking at mountains that had witnessed none of my history. It's amazing the rush of feeling and memories that can be unleashed by such a trigger. My stay in Vietnam was proving to be a time of reflection and of putting some painful memories to rest, and although it was almost ten years ago, I was quite shattered by the poignancy of the images that those mountains had conjured up.

The walk down from the schools had left me melancholy, and on the return to Tien Yen I was quiet. My family that once was so compact and so perfect is now fragmented, and I ache for those years when we were all together. It is an illusion, I know, because children grow and scatter regardless of what happens within the family unit, and I think both Dave's and my genes have contributed to our children's restless need to see more of the world. Natasha, at eighteen, set off on her travels alone, visited the US, Fiji and Australia, and is now making her way through Malaysia and Thailand. Nicko has spent the last two years in Australia and Gerry had one year in New Zealand. As they have grown they have become my friends, and that is as much as a parent can ever dare hope for.

When we got back to Tien Yen, very late on Thursday, I could barely climb my stairs; I felt and looked about a million years old.

Xuan and Mr Trinh left to go back to Hanoi, and Thau plays her music and I sew.

The quilt is nearly finished. It does look quite beautiful and I just pray it does not fall to bits before it gets backed. A Dutch lady in Hanoi is a specialist in quilts, so she and her group of handicapped girls are going to back it for me.

I got an email from Natasha, full of her adventures. She had a motorbike crash in Thailand and then, whilst doing a somersault into the sea in Cambodia, she nearly broke her neck. She sounds undaunted and cheerful; I just cannot wait until she gets here.

Tien Yen

20 March 2002

As I write my letters, I realise I have little control of what each one will contain. Events occur that I could never have predicted, and impressions have been made on me that perhaps have changed my way of thinking for ever. I sometimes feel as though I am outside looking in and the character called Gael is someone else. The changes are subtle and, as I listen to the events that are occurring on the world stage, I know that being lonely and isolated from friends and family ranks very insignificantly against the terrible wrongs that have been committed against the Muslim women of Afghanistan and similar places.

The world has watched news broadcasts of the degradation and lack of human rights that these women have suffered under the Taliban regime. As the weeks passed we heard of the lifting of the veil and a small glimmer of hope being offered to allow them to take their rightful place in society once more.

I watched the CNN news broadcasts in Hanoi and listened to the BBC World Service in Tien Yen. As I watched and listened, it was hard to comprehend that this was really the same century that we were all living in, and I was deeply troubled by the manipulation of the supposed Word of God in the hands of fanatics.

I continue to visit schools and watch and listen to my neighbours and colleagues, but can contribute little as my Vietnamese is still so limited. I try to join in the keep fit class and have attended a few ballroom dancing sessions to show that I am willing to integrate into village life.

I came to Vietnam unsure of what to expect, and my stage has gradually gathered a cast of hundreds, all with one syllable names: Xuan, Bich, Minh, Hang, Trinh. Together we are bound by our shared observations and experiences.

This morning, whilst I was eating *banh my* (bread) and honey and drinking my freshly squeezed orange juice on my little balcony, I was reading *The Tale of Genji*, written by a Japanese writer, Murasaki Skikibu, in the year 1002. She said that she could not bear to let the events that were unfolding around her be lost into oblivion. She was not in an isolated post, visiting schools in the mountains, but was writing about the Imperial Court, where four hundred and thirty courtiers were all involved in some sexual liaison. I could see her point, you would need someone to keep tabs on who was doing what, where, and with whom, but it is my experience that the gossips always do that anyway.

Skikibu described the way a man would court a lady for marriage. The custom was that he would send her a thirty-one-syllable poem and then deduce her character by her reply. No one was expected to be faithful after marriage, but this way of life led to unhappiness because these wonderfully elegant people could not cope with the uncertainty of their relationships and became morbid and jealous. In Japanese society, jealousy was a breach of good manners. They all pined for security but got bored with it. They worried about losing a love, about committing themselves, about the future and about what the gossips might say. So, despite the privilege and the beauty that surrounded them, they were often miserable and melancholy.

I know that many of us are haunted by similar feelings to those she described one thousand years ago. Society may have evolved – we are certainly freer and there is more equality (in some countries) – but the echoes of Bunyan's *Pilgrim's Progress* come back to me. I was sixteen when I first heard about the 'Giant's Cave' and the 'Slough of Despond', and I remember how, as girls, we used to laugh when we had the blues or when the 'black dog' of depression got us. We would say, 'Just leave me, the Giant has me.'

It is still the same today. People still get the blues, and the reasons are often much the same as the Japanese writer described in her record of the Imperial Court. We still pursue rainbows and seek the unattainable, often finding that the pursuit is more exciting than the possession, but somehow, whatever we do, wherever we end up, we are still plagued by the shifting sands of discontent.

The Love Markets in the north of Vietnam bear a striking resemblance to the Imperial Court of Japan in the year 1002, but, not being an anthropologist, I could not comment on the effects on the people involved. They may be riddled with jealousy, they may be trying to 'save face', but the custom has been in place for many years, and these markets are used by the ethnic minority people as a vehicle for social exchange. Xuan told me that these markets function as a way of meeting first your spouse and later others for a bit of variation. An evening is spent on the hillside and then the lovers might spend the night together before returning to their respective families. Sometimes they can be away for a few days. No one seems to expect faithfulness for life, nor, it would seem, even immediately after marriage.

The ethnic Thai men can have more than one wife, but the husband must invite them all to live together in the one house and they all must share the same bed. I can imagine him sitting smoking his cigarettes, sipping his green tea and filing his long nails as his many women tend the fields and the animals.

Perhaps if the women get tense they chew betel nut. The bitter, piquant mix has an intoxicating effect, being a close relative of hashish or marijuana, and has for centuries been regarded by the Vietnamese as a symbol of conjugal fidelity. It quickens the blood circulation, makes a woman's eyes shine, makes her cheeks rosy and reddens her lips. An ideal recipe for a group love-in!

Tien Yen

24 March 2002

Yesterday the most terrible accident happened. A fifty-one-year-old woman was killed by a JCB digger. She had been carrying a very heavy container full of water and, as she passed the construction site where the JCB was gouging out great chunks of earth from the road, she lost her balance and fell down into the path of the machine. Being a bit fat, she was unable to get up before the great bucket with forked prongs came down fast and literally cut her body in two.

Thau and I passed the funeral this morning. The relatives were setting up the tables and chairs in the street at six o'clock, all wearing white bandanas as they set out beer, 7-Up, Fanta and flasks of tea. Everyone is in shock. Thau told me that two youths had also been killed in a motorbike accident, but somehow their tragic deaths have been overshadowed by the unique horror of this one.

Feelings in this town are real; everyone knows everyone else, so the grief of mourning is felt in every shop and in every cluster of squatting people. In the large cities, however, I am told that the services of professional mourners can be bought. They are hired to cry and are required to weep copiously for three or four days as a sign of respect and love for the departed. A professional mourner can receive around VND 1 million (about £50), though as it is only casual work, they are usually housewives or small street vendors who do it to earn a little extra money.

I thought of all this as Thau and I planned our trip to Lang Son. The death has cast a feeling of gloom over the house and our visitors all talk in intense, hushed voices as they retell the story, adding snippets from all possible sources. How the JCB driver was feeling and what the police were doing. As for me, I wish I could make sense of such a terrible death. It certainly made me focus on the Tao religion, which highlights man's insignificance and small role in the great scheme of things. Tao paintings all feature the diminutive size of mortal man in comparison with the great mountains and the forces of nature.

I couldn't help thinking of the fatalistic attitudes that govern people's thinking here in Vietnam and how people walk untroubled and without looking into the busy streets of Hanoi. They are quite cavalier as they gamble with death; '*que sera*'... so why worry? I wonder if that poor woman had any inkling of what was to happen to her; I wonder what her thoughts were?

I am constantly fascinated by the dual personas of the Vietnamese people. There is the aggressive, intrusive, almost downright rude side that is obsessed with amassing huge wads of dong. Yet the incredible beauty of this country is not only in the mountains, rivers and tiered rice fields, but also in the bent backs that work them and the recycling of every piece of waste into something useful. It is the stoic patience and stillness that you see in the faces in doorways and shops and on vendors at the side of the road. It is the fatalistic calmness and attitude to life that is often depicted in Vietnamese poetry; the matter of fact descriptions of pain and suffering alongside beautiful, sensitive imagery.

Whereas the Muslim faith dictates how people should think and behave, the Taoists give reverence instead to nature and to man's part in the great cosmos. The Buddhists put emphasis on the need to perfect oneself, to try to control worldly desires as the path to becoming more generous, patient and wise.

The Vietnamese take a little of everything, including the social hierarchy of Confucianism, and mix it all with the most widespread belief throughout the country, that of Ancestor Worship. There is an altar in the most prestigious place in every home, and it is believed that the soul lives on and protects the living. Thus the memory of the deceased is kept alive in the hearts of those who loved them.

I think I can go along with that.

Thau and I have been busy, visiting schools and distributing clothes in Ba Che district. I was struck again by the dire poverty of some of the families. Young children hang around holding even younger brothers and sisters on their hips, their own schooldays officially over. For food they get little other than rice soup, although there are chickens and pigs running about, as the animals are only reared in order to be sold in the market. A typical family's rice harvest yields about VND three million (£150) a year. From that income so many expenses have to be met, and education is not the number one priority. I was beginning to see Bich's plans for raising rabbits as a dietary supplement without my usual sentimentality. I just wish she hadn't chosen the big white flopsy variety.

Tien Yen, 25 March 2002

My dear Gerry,

The quilt is finished!

I sat all afternoon unpicking the newspaper hexagons that formed the patterns for the slippery silk. Each piece had been patiently pinned then tacked on, and now the over-sewing is complete. The quilt looks fragile and flimsy without its backing. I am covered in bits of thread and there is a huge pyramid of paper depicting scraps of news of the last six months. Items from the headlines, Bin Laden, Taliban, George W Bush; pieces of unfinished crosswords; and a sea of words that I don't understand.

Thau is busy learning how to use the SCF digital camera and is photographing everything in sight. She came into my room very proudly with a beautiful portrait of a hairy Highland cow that she had snapped from my Scottish calendar. She is going to photograph The Great Work and will put it on the computer; I shall send it on to you so you can see what I have been up to all this time.

It has been more than just a hobby and more than a means of keeping sane. It has helped me to focus my thoughts and, at the same time, kept me involved and physically present. I may not have been able to contribute to the chatty evening conversations, but the fact that I was there meant that I was not rejecting the group by going off alone to my room to read, and so isolating myself from them. As a result it has been a life-saver as well as another channel of communication, for the teachers, lecturers and visitors have all admired it and many have actually contributed and sewn or tacked a piece in.

Anyway, it is now done and you will see it soon. The next step will be to get it backed in Hanoi. I am so pleased with myself!

Love Mum

Tien Yen

26 March 2002

Mr Trinh was away for the weekend in Hanoi, so Thau and I decided to act on our plan of going to Lang Son, the main border crossing to China. We caught the local bus and drove northwest for four horrendous hours along a dirt track. This connects with the super duper new highway number 4 that runs from Lang Son to Hanoi, linking up with highway number 1 that goes south, like a great artery, to Ho Chi Minh City. Cartographers in Vietnam are struggling to keep up with the developments as, from north to south, new roads are being carved through mountains and forests and travellers are experiencing a new era of speed and efficiency as the infrastructure joins the twenty-first century.

I wondered at our sanity as we bounced over the potholes and inhaled the dust that enveloped the bus. The driver had no concept of 'we're full' and instead stopped continually to let more and more of humanity on board, plus their cargo. Admittedly it was worse on the way back, as I sat with my legs astride the biggest bag bulging with badminton rackets, manicure sets, bras and about a ten-year supply of knickers. These cheap goods from China go to stock up local shops, and farmers and householders bring back fertiliser, rice and mobile generators. Thank goodness we had no animals in our bus, and none on the roof-rack either.

The communal toilet stop was a definite no-no. If I could I would have crossed my legs, for there was no way that I was going for a 'ladies squat together behind a bush' party. And as for the men... need I say more? The firing squad could have just picked off the line of backs watering the roadside. They looked as though they were waiting to be shot as they stood shoulder to shoulder with their heads bent down, all concentrating together. Fortunately Thau and I were able to find relief at a local shop, under the pretext of stopping to buy water.

As the journey unfolded, we passed through such beautiful countryside, rolling mountains, villages, rivers, and miles and miles of rice fields nestled into the foothills of the mountains. I had to smile when I saw a buffalo ploughing through a paddy field, followed by a whole platoon of brown hens marching along in military style behind it.

We got into Lang Son, were whipped away by waiting *xe om* drivers, and settled into a clean, central hotel. We had our Lonely Planet guidebook with us and, faithfully following all the advice, literally visited just about every sight. We took a minibus to the border and saw the longest queue of trucks in the world… beating even the '*bouchons*' in France when the Dutch and the British head south each summer to the Mediterranean.

I have memories of being stuck in the heat alongside huge container trucks, all heading to Spain, and the hours ticking slowly by as whatever had caused the hold-up was cleared. In Lang Son the drivers had slung hammocks under their lorries and were sleeping away the time, or reading the newspaper or just being social and exchanging a cigarette or cup of tea. It looked so cool and comfortable and so sensible. I asked a group playing cards what their cargo was. They told us it was mostly fruit from the south of Vietnam going to China, and they normally have to wait a day to get processed through customs. They play cards as the officials go through all the red tape, although I am told that a little money helps the process. I was intrigued as I know there is a lot of child trafficking going on, and I couldn't help looking at the trucks and wondering.

The border itself was like a scene from a Cold War movie. Police, guards and officials all patrolled. Men in military uniforms sat behind desks and flicked through passports and documents. With so much paperwork, how did twenty-two thousand women and children get through these borders over the last eight years as part of the lucrative and growing human trade?

The trafficking of Vietnamese children and women to neighbouring countries is on the increase. The whole business is hidden from sight and is beyond the reach of the law as young girls are forced to marry Chinese men and are then set to work as prostitutes. Owing to the illicit nature of the business, little is known about trafficked children and those who enslave them. I remember reading a report about this in the SCF office; it indicated that the children typically came from poor provinces where parents were normally offered a few hundred dollars and a guarantee that their child would get a well-paid job. Instead, the reality is that the children are promptly deprived of their identity papers and forced into slavery.

Some children do manage to escape and make their way back across the border, and here in Lang Son there is a transition centre, run by the Women's Union, where children and women are cared for while the police investigate their background. Unfortunately the procedure is lengthy and the red tape, lack of documentation and trauma add to the fear and humiliation that these trafficked children have already been exposed to.

As I stood and looked at the officials, I did wonder whether they took money as bribes or respected the agreement of cooperation that had been set down in Bangkok by the six nations, Thailand, Cambodia, Laos, Vietnam, Myanmar and China. They had agreed to ensure that existing laws were used to protect victims of trafficking and not to punish them as illegal migrants.

I had heard stories of girls as young as fourteen being returned to their native countries after working as prostitutes in Bangkok. Because they had contracted the AIDS virus they were subsequently put to death by lethal injection. A child's life is cheap and easily reproduced. There is no thought given to words such as dignity or to humanitarian values. It would seem that business and money are the greatest motivators in our global society, and the trafficking of children into prostitution has become the world's most lucrative illegal trade after drugs and arms smuggling.

I recall looking down the busy main streets of the cities of Aberdeen, Glasgow and Edinburgh, wondering how many people amongst the thronging masses were at that moment suffering from cancer or attending clinics for some slow, debilitating disease. The faces in the crowd gave nothing away; all looked blank and anonymous, with personal stories carefully hidden behind impassive masks; only the clothes flaunted personal tastes that might signal individuality, or not.

Today I would look again at those streets and wonder, not at the human frailties and sufferings, but at the faces that mask the cold, cruel streak that can cause so much pain to supposed loved ones and vicious intolerance towards those that are different. This calculated hatred or mindless indifference seems to permeate all communities throughout the world. Like ill health or unhappiness, it can be so cleverly hidden, and I wonder what happened to the hippie cry of the 1960s that echoed the teaching of a Jewish carpenter 2000 years ago: 'Love thy neighbour, and do unto others as you would have them do unto you'.

From the greater stage of the evils and wrongs in the world, I focussed again on the specific image of the trucks and border patrols and the particular issue of child trafficking. Would the quiet voices of reason that speak on behalf of the great mass of silent victims be heard against the cash till that only recognises the sign of the dollar? We can only hope. In the meantime, I looked at Thau and wondered how much I would get for her!

Back in town we visited the caves, huge natural grottos in the limestone monoliths. Buddhist shrines nestle in all the nooks and crannies, so we dutifully lit incense and prayed. One cave reminded me so much of the huge cathedrals of Antwerp and Rome, cool and cavernous, and, as you look way up, the rock is slightly open and you can see the sky in the distance. Like the Renaissance artists, this natural phenomenon forces our eyes up towards the light and so to God. The way the rock seemed to be spilling over into globby, almost fluid shapes reminded me of Gaudi's Sagrada Familia cathedral in Barcelona.

Thau and I just stood in awe. With the events of the last few days and the funeral of our neighbour, my thoughts have been turning to religion, and now here I was looking up to God in a cave in Vietnam. Suddenly I was full of reflection on the Christian faith that had moulded me and had provided the inspiration and motivation, as well as a genre, for so many great artists, sculptors and musicians of the West.

We did see another interesting phenomenon. It was a rock, high on a hill, that resembles, from a distance, a woman holding a child. The local legend is that she stands looking towards the hills of China, eternally waiting for her soldier husband to return. He never did... or will. Very poignant.

After the dusty journey and all the sightseeing, we decided to have our hair washed, in the usual dentist chair with a red plastic bowl, but this time in a 'bride's shop'. It seemed so bizarre getting all the ingrained red dust scrubbed out of our heads and our faces massaged whilst surrounded by white crinoline dresses.

We returned to Tien Yen by the same bus and with the same driver. Thau had developed a little crush on him, as he had a shy smile and wore a green pith helmet. A few months later she told me she had seen him at the local discotheque and didn't recognise him without his hat, but then she saw his bus parked outside and all became clear.

Our two-day trip was exhausting and we felt as though we had been away for weeks. I have some photos of us as tourists, but there were many images that I could not record with my camera, as sometimes it is just too intrusive. Everywhere I go I am as much a curiosity to the people I meet as they are to me. I have been so lucky having Xuan and now Thau, and so am able to talk to everyone I come across. The images that aren't captured by Kodak can be recalled by smell, a piece of music or a chance word; they are never lost.

Watermelons will always remind me of my trip to the Chinese border. On the way to the border, I saw a group of children mucking about with about twenty discarded melons. A couple of girls had stuffed their feet into two melons and were trying to walk as though on stilts. Imagine the sensation – it must have been heavenly. Boys were chucking the melons about and the road looked like a red battleground... a stark reminder that this was where China invaded Vietnam in 1979, but unwisely had not reckoned on the Vietnamese powers of resilience. The Chinese were pushed back after three weeks of fighting with tens of thousands dead. True figures were concealed by both governments and several towns were destroyed.

Hanoi

27 March 2002

It is nice to be back in Hanoi, and I have been a whirlwind of efficiency: exchanging books, taking the quilt on its final journey to get backed and visiting friends. I am so excited as I am going to meet Natasha in the next few days as she is due up from Hue. It is such a wonderful feeling, knowing that she will be arriving soon, and I can't wait to meet Richard tomorrow.

Hanoi

28 March 2002

I met Richard again. I had been so excited about seeing him, and my stomach just flipped when I saw him sitting in the reception area of my hotel. He didn't even raise his head when I said hello. We ate and drank and rode around on his motorbike. I could sense that the relationship that was founded on mutual need in December was now imbalanced. He has a new job and, quite naturally, he has established a new network of friends. I sat and looked and listened. I understood. I looked at his face and thought of all the daydreams that I had had during the lonely days in Tien Yen, and how he had been like a thread that had woven strands of silver and gold through these last few months.

By verbalising all my inner thoughts and confusions to Richard, he had acted as the catalyst that I needed in order to question my decisions and my future choices. I loved my job, but there were too many days with too little to do, and I needed people that I could easily communicate with. I made a decision to leave VSO, and Bill at Save the Children supported my decision. He understood the isolation and he knew that I had given as much as I could to the project. I would leave at the end of the academic year, go home to Edinburgh for a few months, and then come back and start my new job at the United Nations International School in Hanoi, where I would be a class teacher for Grade 1.

I had wanted to celebrate my new appointment with Richard, share my excitement about Natasha's imminent arrival and tell him about all the events that had happened in Tien Yen. Instead I looked at him across the table and realised he had no interest whatsoever.

We said we would stay friends, and I suppose we have.

Balcony, Hang Gai Street, Hanoi
July 2002

The relationship did continue for the next few months. Richard continued to stress that he wanted no commitment, and yet he could not deny the easy friendship and warmth that came from us being together. I used to do crossword puzzles and he would watch TV. I just loved being with him; it didn't really matter what we did. I remember the afternoons when we rode through the emerald patchwork of rice along the Red River or through the dusty towns and villages outside Hanoi. I would rest my cheek on his back and hold him in my arms and let all the magic of the scenery roll in front of my eyes. Dragonflies bombarded us on the motorbike as we watched flocks of ducks being led at dusk from the lakes, waddling up the sides of the dykes like a white waterfall in reverse. The sun would set and cooking smells would float up from wood burning stoves. We would return to the city and he would leave me, and I would be filled again with a sense of loss and emptiness.

Natasha arrived at the end of March. She bounced into my hotel room, so full of energy and vitality and so tall, deeply tanned and quite beautiful. She was more than a link with home, she was a dynamo, and she filled my life with energy and enthusiasm once again. Now when I walk around Hanoi I sometimes feel a lump in my throat and have to squeeze my eyes shut as I remember all the walking and sightseeing and shopping we did. I remember her rowing me on a little boat on West Lake… it was such a lazy afternoon. I took a photograph of her in her orange T-shirt; she was so pretty with her hair escaping from her ponytail, just little wisps around her face. It sits in my kitchen here, under the watchful gaze of the giant poster of Ho Chi Minh.

Everyone at Save the Children made her so welcome, and she came and stayed with me in Tien Yen. We had a training session immediately after getting back from Hanoi and she helped me prepare materials for these events. Her artwork has been faithfully and repeatedly copied and now adorns the shabby walls of so many classrooms.

Tien Yen

4 April 2002

It has been so good having Natasha here; her presence has changed the dynamics of the office and suddenly youth rules! All her CDs are played, so we have had a rest from 'My Love' and 'Solida'. She, Thau and Hiep talk music and fashion and compare different trends of the different cultures. They are planning to go to the discotheque tonight. I have warned her about the cha-cha, but I don't think she believes me.

Hang is entranced with Natasha's height, and keeps miming behind her back at the huge difference between them, but there is a bond there already; Natasha just loves Hang's cooking and sometimes helps her to chop vegetables. Xuan, Trinh and I had to sample one of the recipes that she and Hang had so painstakingly made together. They had been to the market and came back laden with tofu, pork mince and assorted leaves. I was intrigued when they mixed the mince with chopped onions, pepper and a spoonful of fish sauce. After chopping the tofu into rectangles they cut these into halves, stuffed them with the meat mixture and deep fried them until golden. Whilst Natasha was doing this, Hang fried some tomatoes, fish sauce and oil together, then poured this over the tofu and sprinkled it all with coriander leaves. The smell was wonderful and, eaten with rice, it was just *ngon lam*.

Although Natasha helped to clear up the plates, I didn't notice her helping to wash the dishes. Hang squats by a cold pipe, lathers each plate and scours it with an abrasive cloth. She sits amidst all the debris with the water running and everything is completed in her own efficient way. She then loads all the plates and cutlery on to the table, turns up the fan to its highest speed and goes off to gossip with her friends.

Natasha has been using the office motorbike to go exploring in the afternoon and has been down all the roads leading out of Tien Yen, including the long winding one that follows the river the ten kilometres to the sea at Mui Chua. She left the bike and picked her way along the rocky shoreline to a flat rock under a straggly tree. Later she told me she knew that we had been there, as the evidence of the orange peel still remained. The crabs, no doubt, would have demolished the meat and breadcrumbs we had also left.

Mr Trinh has unofficially adopted Natasha and keeps her bowl constantly filled with crab, prawns and pork. He chuckles and laughs and keeps talking about daughters-in-law. I think Xuan, Thau and I are secretly quite jealous. He seems to have forgotten us, so let's hope this infatuation is only temporary.

The teachers love her in the training sessions, and hug her and smooth her arms and back and chatter amongst themselves. After work we have taken to wandering down the street and usually end up at the river. We sit where I used to take Mr Darcy and watch the scenes of the evening. The beauty of this particular sight – sunset on a river – is universal in Asia and has been painted and photographed by so many that have seen it. As a consequence, the scene is no longer unique, but almost bland and familiar, as a Scottish castle is on a tin of Scottish shortbread.

This is the time when fishing boats return and sampans unload their creaking, worn out baskets full of fish the size of small sprats. They tie up in convoys and their owners leap from boat to boat, black stick men with conical hats silhouetted against the saffron streaks of the setting sun. On the river bank, crowded clusters of shacks lose their look of hovels and dirty middens, for their irregular tin roofs frame the sky in a sharp and pleasing contrast to the sky's luminous colours before the downfall of the blanket of darkness.

It is a busy time and Natasha and I watched as bicycles and motorbikes 'peeped' their way home, people prepared supper, and, from above, the wretched loudspeakers blasted music, songs and news bulletins.

We have been sitting on my little balcony drinking Hanoi beer and eating mangoes in the evenings, and I try not to focus on the total destruction of my neat and tidy room behind me. How has one girl caused so much havoc? A bomb or a robber could not have made so much mess. I bite my tongue as I know my nest will return to its pristine state when my bird flies off. Clothes, books, make-up, diaries, photographs lie in a wild confusion on the floor and on every surface. As she chatters on about her travels, I cannot help feeling rather foolish for having worried so much about her. I remember lecturing her at the airport in Edinburgh, almost a year ago, about the dangers of rape drugs, dodgy straws and evil men. Instead, strewn across the floor are photos of smiley faces, bronzed Adonises and gorgeous girls. Temples, orang-utans, silvery sands and turquoise seas, lime-green bikinis and shimmery yachts. Why had I worried? She has had the most wonderful adventure, had coped with all the little set-backs, and was now sitting in Tien Yen, dripping mango juice without a care in the world.

I remember when she was little. I had taken the three of them to London for half-term. Coming out of the theatre after seeing Cats I did not know how to get to Baker Street, and felt very 'Highland' and lost. Eventually we made it and were sitting on the train bound for Amersham when she held my hand and said, 'I hate it when you don't know what to do.' Somehow I cannot imagine her being lost anywhere.

Tien Yen
7 April 2002

Last night was the end of the training, and after dinner everyone assembled in the training room. I looked around at the forty teachers, the ladies from the Ministry of Education in Hanoi and Xuan, and it dawned on me that this would be the last time that we would all be together. The school year finishes at the end of May and that is when I shall be leaving. The teachers have grown in confidence and the trainers from the Ministry, Oanh and Hoa, are now using my methods. Oanh hopes to come up to Tien Yen in order to visit the teachers in situ, just to reinforce practices and give encouragement. They sang all the songs that have become so familiar, and I can still hear the great swell of sound as they lifted the notes, high and clear and pure:

> *Trai bau xanh, trai bi xanh*
> *Theo gio trong lanh cat tieng hat vui chung*
> *Bau oi thuong lay bi cung*
> *Tuy rang khac giong nhung chung mot gian*
> *Bau oi thuong lay bi cung*
> *Tuy rang khac giong nhung chung mot gian.*

(A green squash and a green pumpkin
Are singing in the wind,
they sing songs of love together
Because they know they come
From the same family.)

Natasha and I sang:

Come by the hills, to the land where fancy is free,
And stand where the peaks meet the sky
And the rocks meet the sea,
Where the rivers run clear,
And the bracken is gold in the sun,
And the cares of tomorrow must wait,
'Til this day is done.

The teachers clapped and looked bemused, then there were more Vietnamese songs and finally it was over.

Today I went into the training room to clear up materials and felt such a pang of sadness. The house is quiet again. Hang is mopping and the car has gone.

Tien Yen

12 April 2002

Mr Trinh arrived with the first batch of rabbits, and he and Hiep took them to a couple of communes in Dong Ngu. Although I can understand the thinking behind Bich's great plan, I just wish that they had chosen a more Watership Down kind of rabbit instead of the standard white flopsy bunny that one normally associates eating carrots in a hutch in the back garden.

We have been busy visiting schools and must have walked so many miles. To get to one school we had to cross a river on a small boat operated by a wire pulley system. I hate to think what would have happened if the river was in full spate, as our operator was a frail-looking, skinny old man with a tiny knot in his arm that I presume was a muscle.

One afternoon, in order to help share skills, we brought some of the weaker teachers to visit one of our stars, Tam, the teacher from Dong Son. She did a demonstration lesson and afterwards Oanh led a discussion. It must have been quite traumatic for Tam to teach in front of the trainers, but she is such a good teacher and she looked so confident. I am sure her audience would have learnt from their afternoon and so be inspired when they returned to their own schools.

As we drove back to Tien Yen, I couldn't help reflecting how the teaching methods had progressed from the initial training sessions of 'chalk and talk'. Xuan and I introduced a film and a book that we had produced using photographs with simple captions to highlight good practice, and now we were confident enough to bring others to watch Tam demonstrate all these ideas.

Tien Yen
14 April 2002

Well, I have seen starry skies before, but on Friday night Galileo would not have bothered making his telescope if he had been with me. The stars were so clear and almost touchable, and the great Professor Tasha pointed out Scorpio for me. I felt such a dreamer as I walked in the pitch black, gazing upwards, when I had the very nice sensation of walking into a very large pile of buffalo poo.

My mood was reflective and, as I walked, I thought of the past two weeks of training teachers and visiting schools. There are so many different levels of competence and it is important to focus on the methods of teaching, but the common factor in each school is always the same shy children with floppy black hair, wearing ragged shirts and sitting on dusty floors. It doesn't take long before you are rewarded with a tentative smile as you sit down on the floor with them and start playing with cubes or drawing pictures; the teacher then relaxes and the horrible feeling of 'inspection' goes.

I have persuaded them of the benefits of working in groups, thus most of the teachers have divided their children according to age or ability. Now we see maths games, drawing, writing and Plasticine all going on at once. These are the same girls that were dismissed by the Ministry trainers last September as being totally unsuitable. The biggest obstacle is the girls who use their ethnic language to communicate, as the children do not make any progress with their Vietnamese. It is rather like me having Xuan and Thau to translate; there is little need to learn.

On Friday evening Mr Trinh drove us to Halou Commune and left us there for the night. The headmaster invited us for dinner at the main school and his wife served us boiled chicken and rice wine; at the end of the meal everyone felt very affectionate towards everyone else. The Vietnamese love to touch and groom each other constantly, but only the same sex, and I am now getting used to my legs, arms and back being caressed by other women as I speak. I shall have to relearn how to behave when I go back to Edinburgh.

After dinner we set off to cross the river by the latest great feat of engineering, the New Bridge. It was literally two trees suspended on five oil drums that had been dug into the riverbed. Of course there was no handrail, so the crossing was slow and precarious, even with bravado and the Dutch courage from the wine drunk at dinner.

It was about eight o'clock when we met up in the preschool teacher's house. The small hamlet did have light as electricity was generated from the river and transmitted up to the houses along a spaghetti mess of wires, all at about mid-chest level. It was a total nightmare to negotiate the path with only one pathetically small torch.

The atmosphere in the house reminded me of Tet or a Scottish New Year, as all the extended family and neighbours had called in to check out the aliens. Everyone was very interested in our ages and marital status; they found all our answers hilarious and laughed and laughed.

We drank tea, and then the three teachers, Xuan, Thau, Tasha and I set off to hunt for snails. We made our way to the river and waded in. Two of us were fire bearers, holding aloft burning bamboo torches. The others were bent double, engrossed, while hands explored all the rocks and stones and grabbed the slippery, unsuspecting but surprisingly fast little creatures.

After the initial mirth, it all became quite quiet and, during my time as the 'light giver', I just gazed at the sky and the river and the women with their bent backs and listened to the sloshing sounds of the water going over the rocks. Apart from our two sources of flaming light, the night was pitch black. From above our figures would have been invisible; there was by now no light at all from the tiny village and no large town or settlement for miles and miles. We were completely isolated and I was conscious of being part of the rhythm of a way of life that had been going on, uninterrupted, for thousands of years.

We parted at around ten o'clock and the houses we passed had obviously gone to sleep, so we struggled back to our crossing place by starlight. This time we had no qualms about getting our feet wet and wisely avoided the great feat of engineering as we made our way back to the school where we were to spend the night. We all shared beds in one of the teacher's rooms, and lay under our nets by candlelight until we slept. It was not for long, however, as the day here begins before five (according to the cockerels).

So much for my morning rituals of shower and make-up application. I just struggled into yesterday's clothes, sucked some toothpaste and staggered off for some bread and water. I did get a lovely surprise when the headmaster produced some Nescafé sachets, but then he brought down a big flagon of dark brown liquid with half a forest floating in it and poured me a glass. It is supposed to be good for health and digestion but, when I sipped it, the alcohol nearly blew my head off.

Mr Trinh arrived at about half past six and we set off even further into the no-man's land of rural isolation and came across the most idyllic village. Xuan went off for a meeting with the Chief of the village, a very strict communist. The People's Committees tolerate charities like SCF but, in reality, we all have doubts about the sustainability of our efforts. Without donations of resources from the charities, the children would have nothing, and, with the new government policy of stopping the subsidising of schools in the ethnic minority regions, parents cannot and will not be able to afford textbooks to support the new curriculum for their children. Many have large families so the situation in the next few years looks grim.

When Xuan was a girl she lived in an equally poor area in the province of Son La, but at that time the government's policy was to subsidise all schools so that all children had an equal chance. Now, since perestroika or, in Vietnam, Doi Moi, and the resulting new market economy, people are being encouraged to work for themselves. Thus, like everywhere else in the world the rich are getting richer and there is not much hope for the poor. Xuan and her sister were both able to study and get into university in Hanoi. It will be an utter miracle if any of the children that I am involved with ever even finish primary school. We've talked to some of the older children that come and hang around the preschools when we visit; many are now aged about eleven or twelve and have left school already. They may have only finished Grade 3 but their parents either needed them to care for the buffalo or younger siblings or simply just could not afford the expense of further schooling.

That may explain why there is a market for the sale of girls to China. They are sent to be wives or prostitutes as China has made such a mess of their population. The Asian culture emphasises the importance of a male descendant and allegedly there have been thousands of girl children lost to infanticide as a direct result of the Chinese government's policy of limiting birth rates to one child per family. There are far too many boys in China and there are now two generations of men that need women. Girls from other countries in Southeast Asia are sent supposedly to right this imbalance.

I have digressed again from the school we were visiting. We arrived to find the young teacher was teaching her children about stones and bricks. I watched her for a while but as it was so tedious I asked Natasha to quickly draw me the story of the *Three Little Pigs*. Using that aid, I then told the story with all the huffing and puffing and body language, and Thau translated using very simple words. The children's faces were such a picture. We made bricks with Plasticine and drew houses, and when the teacher retold the story the children clearly understood the new words. By this stage the children had relaxed after the intrusion of the visitors and sang us songs; some even sang solos. It was amazing as, just an hour before, I doubted they would do anything since they were so withdrawn and shy.

I can still see Natasha and Thau sitting on the floor, their backs leaning against the wall, learning how to make buffaloes out of jackfruit leaves. The children were leaning against them and their small black heads crowded in as thread was pulled through to make the 'head with the horns' lift up and down and a 'mooing' noise was made.

We met up with Xuan and had lunch with another teacher and the Chief of the village. It was boiled chicken, of course, with sticky rice and some sort of pickled vegetable. The men got utterly blitzed on rice wine, but thank God Mr Trinh only had one glass before retiring to the bed next to the table, where he lay smoking his cigarette and picking his toes. It was all so relaxed.

Inevitably nature called and I enquired where the toilet was. At the side of the house there was a fence made of bamboo, and, through the gate, there were a few pens that had a pig in one and some ducks in another. The third one had a fertiliser bag draped in front of it, and I was shown into that. The floor was just open slats of rounded bamboo, and there was a chicken roosting on the sidewall. As I was left alone there, a whole gaggle of geese appeared and eyed me through the woven latticework wall. Basic human functions obviously require little privacy, so I just had to get on with it.

We got back to Tien Yen late in the afternoon, and all of us rushed for the shower. We were tired and sat sipping tea as Hang brought us up to date with the news of the town. I remember when I used to think living in Tien Yen was difficult.

Tien Yen

16 April 2002

There is a new sign up outside Minh's. It is white with red writing, and apparently it is advertising the new aerobics classes. The first starts at five in the morning, the last ends at ten at night, so there is really no excuse not to attend, as surely there must be a time that would be suitable for everyone. Natasha and I decided to go along to the latest class. When I went in I really could not believe this was the same place as that small, cramped bedroom that we had started out in. The room was huge, with beautiful blue tiles on the floor, a huge dance mirror, hooks with a job lot of new leotards hanging on them, and the ladies of the Keep Fit were a spectacle to behold in their body-hugging lycra. Minh was a new woman, still the queen bee with all her attendants buzzing around her, squeezing each other's loose bits or going for close-up comparisons in front of the large mirror. They looked over their shoulders as they tried to assess their bums, glared fiercely at the mirror as they sucked in their round stomachs. When they were quite happy with the full inspection they would focus on their faces, twitch from side to side and rearrange their hair. They were ready.

A TV and VCR had been installed, so Tasha and I presumed that we would all be watching the Vietnamese equivalent of Jane Fonda and just get on with it. Not so. We all watched in anticipation, but then Minh turned off the tape and proceeded to teach us herself. It was painfully slow as she went over the same little steps and hops over and over again, concentrating a lot on arm movements. Natasha and I were entranced and obediently followed her actions, trying not to notice the huge throng of onlookers at the door. The 'lads' were back, so I was very glad that we had not been talked into wearing some skinny little swimsuit thing.

The session was a study in concentration until Minh with her beady eyes noticed someone doing something wrong. Then, like a good teacher trained in positive reinforcement and psychology, she pointed her finger, threw her head back and gave a huge, long cackle. At the end of her 'work-out' Minh turned on Westlife very loudly and ordered us all to dance to 'My Love' and 'Solida'. Natasha and I jiggled about and just could not look at each other. The other ladies seemed untroubled by it all and flamboyantly danced around the room.

From snail-picking in the middle of nowhere to that room where all of the twentieth century seemed to have been encapsulated! I was glad to get back to my own little room and was even more glad that I had my daughter with me.

Time is running out for her, and she has been frantically painting me pictures so that I can get them laminated in Hanoi to use in the schools here and then later in the International School. She has been sorting and tidying and the rucksack is now being repacked because, after our short trip to Halong Bay tomorrow, she will be leaving for Bangkok and then onwards to Scotland. I think she has mixed feelings and is reluctant to leave, but is also impatient to see her friends again; it will almost be a year since she left.

Tien Yen
26 April 2002

It's been a busy week with visits to Ba Che. After a long gruelling drive over the rough terrain it was heavenly to stand in the river that flowed just below the school and let the water wash off the red dust that seems to ingrain itself into our skin. We stood on the rocks and watched the children splashing and swimming with the buffaloes and felt such a twinge of envy as we listened to their shouts and laughter. On each of the stones at our feet were black velvet butterflies with blotches of royal blue on their wings. I wondered what had possessed them to alight there amongst all this noise and confusion, and even as we started to step on the rocks in order to cross they seemed reluctant to fly off.

The teacher was ill, which explained the children's apparent freedom, but she did make the effort to open her classroom for us to see all her handiwork. It was lovely, and models had been set up displaying diggers and other great devices made from Meccano. She was pale so we let her go and rest and instead we drove on to visit the school that we had been to last October on my birthday. On that day we had been treated to speeches, the classroom wall had been draped in a red sheet and Uncle Ho had been centre stage. I remember being charmed at the children's lack of inhibitions as they sang for us and later sitting in the tiny classroom being served with platters of melon, oranges, and mangoes.

Hoa, the teacher, was wonderful. She was so proud as she showed us all the progress that had been made over the last few months. The children performed a drama of *The Enormous Turnip*, and then sang, and showed us Plasticine models of animals and flowers that they were able to name. They seemed so open and friendly and Thau told me that the standard of Vietnamese the children spoke was very good. Going back in the car I was really sad, for this would probably be my last visit to Ba Che.

Hang had made Natasha a wonderful farewell dinner. That night we ate by candlelight and Mr Trinh was even more attentive than usual.

I have been ill. I cannot walk without the fear of falling to one side, feel constantly dizzy and have been popping pills for headaches.

Tomorrow we leave for Hanoi as we have to prepare things in the office for Princess Anne's arrival. Natasha only has a few days left before she leaves for Scotland.

Hanoi

28 April 2002

Last night I went out with Richard. He was like the walking wounded, his big toe encased in a white dressing after a motorbike accident and his body contorted after falling off a bar stool and bruising his coccyx. He was enjoying his misery and I couldn't stop laughing as he recounted all his woes.

We ate and drank, then he lay stretched out on the cushions of Highway 4, a rice wine bar, like some sheikh or pasha. I had to explain to the waiter that he was not actually drunk but that he had a back problem. He sat on the motorbike at an angle, and, sitting behind him, I had visions of us both falling off.

Hanoi

1 May 2002

Natasha left yesterday and I feel bereft. I got back to the hotel and found the SCF girls had put flowers in my room as they knew I would be sad. I was, and wandered around the streets and missed her so much.

A city comes alive when you share it with someone else. When I am on my own I can only observe, and coffees and drinks are just something to do as you watch others laughing and talking. Sometimes it's fun just to watch people, but sometimes it makes me melancholy and sad, and I wish so much that I had someone to do things with.

I realise this is a natural reaction, for I have had Natasha with me for a month and now I am alone. Although I shall see Richard, it seems it will be just on his terms. I cannot stop the tears that start up as I walk by the lake.

Hanoi

5 May 2002

I am not well. I have blinding headaches and I keep losing my balance. Walking down the street I feel so vulnerable and am constantly afraid that I am going to fall to one side. I have been to the doctor and he has confirmed that I have labyrinthitis; there's not much to be done as it is a viral infection of the inner ear. Maybe I contracted it when I dived off the boat and swam in Halong Bay with Natasha. I seem to have been having bad headaches since then.

I am very excited as I have found an apartment to rent. After looking at several houses in various locations around the International School with an agent I have chosen an apartment in Hang Gai Street in the heart of the Old Quarter. When I walked in I just knew that it was right. It has high ceilings, arched windows and is a haven perched above the busy street below. The Old Quarter in Hanoi is a maze of organised confusion; colour, noises and smells all rise up and assault the senses.

When I first arrived I followed my guidebook's instructions and walked through the warren of thirty-six streets, each one specialising in a particular trade that may once have been representatives of the guilds employed by the Emperor. I followed the route and saw streets that specialise in tin boxes, wrought iron windows and gates, traditional medicines, musical instruments, wood and lacquerware, and, in one street, wonderful paper decorations, tinsel, lanterns and kites. Everything is gaudy and colourful and there is an atmosphere of permanent celebration.

I have walked through these streets at night, when all is silent and only the moonlight casts shadows over the clean and deserted pavements. The architecture takes centre stage and the classic French style of the building designs once again becomes apparent. As you walk your eyes are drawn to the beautiful carved doorways and ornate shutters. Above, the ghostly modern additions to the already complicated rooftops mingle with the silhouettes of mature trees and vibrant bougainvillaea that have taken on the black hues of midnight.

It could all be a pen and ink sketch for, here in the heart of the city by moonlight, the streets take on a beauty they do not possess in the afternoon sun.

Hang Gai Street is like the Bond Street of Hanoi, and the silk shops vie against each other, showing pictures of famous customers framed in their windows; Hillary Clinton, Gerard Depardieu, Catherine Deneuve and Queen Sophia of Spain. My new home is an old apartment, two floors up from all this shopping madness, and as I looked at it there seemed to be an aura of the French colonial mixed with Bohemian styles. I felt it was ideal and would suit my new life in Hanoi. It seemed to encompass the very heart of the city, and my closeness to my neighbours ensured day to day contact with Vietnamese families.

I walked back along the lake and sat in a café and ordered fresh lime juice. I watched the tourists passing by and remembered sitting in exactly the same place when I first arrived, first with Emma and Clare and then later on Valentine's Day with Richard. I felt happy and, although I would be leaving VSO, I knew it was not yet time to go home and that I had something more to accomplish in this country. I came out with no expectations; it was almost as though I was starting out on a white canvas. And now, instead of returning to Edinburgh, I feel there is something waiting for me here that I have yet to find.

Hanoi, 6 May 2002

My dear Gerry,

I have been thinking about you all day today; it's funny how when I see things I just want to share them with you and imagine it all through your eyes. This morning I took a xe om out to see Agneta; my driver weaved through the streets, which were less frenetic somehow, so I had the opportunity to see all the day-to-day rituals going on in the shop-houses. People just squat on the pavement and chat to each other, so walkers then have to step on to the road in order to pass. School kids sit and do their homework amidst a busy eating shop, and everyone seems to talk talk talk non-stop.

At Hoc Ngoc Khanh I asked my driver to stop so that I could walk to Agneta's house. I turned off the busy road into a street that meanders around such a pretty lake with baby willows planted at regular intervals around the edge. The branches were so light that they seemed to be dancing and created a green haze of feathery movement. I almost expected to hear a few strains of Tchaikovsky, and standing transfixed I couldn't believe such a serene enclave could exist in such a busy city.

As I walked towards the lake I saw that the whole expanse of water was vibrating and I had to rub my eyes to convince myself that it wasn't me! The effect on the surface of the water was the same as when there is a downpour of monsoon rain. When I looked closer, thousands upon thousands of gold fish were 'hanging' vertically in the water, almost dancing to the same rhythm, and their mouths were gasping for air! I wondered if they were tame and were waiting to be fed or if the water was so polluted that they were all in fact in their death throes.

Over coffee Agneta told me that at night along the roadside of this lake, little plastic tables and chairs appear and the lovers of the neighbourhood meet for private trysts. The local residents make a little business by selling tea and soft drinks and dishes of melon seeds.

Later as I left Agneta's house I was reminded of the movie Oliver, for from around the corner came the most beautiful singing. 'Hay mua banh my di (please buy my bread), banh my nong don day (hot crispy bread),' sang the lowly street vendor in the most wonderful contralto voice as she patrolled the streets with her shoulder pole and her wares balanced in baskets. Her lovely voice was heard until she disappeared, but then another and another came and the sopranos mingled with the altos and occasionally a tenor passed offering to sharpen knives. I floated back to town feeling very relaxed. I had enjoyed some nice company, some David Attenborough nature encounters and live street musical productions!

I went to have my hair cut at my usual ladies' 'salon'. As I waited I couldn't help noticing her display of hair treatment products. The main brand seemed to be not Revlon or Paul Mitchell but 'Bed Head'. The conditioner was labelled 'Control Freak' and the shampoo seemed to be only for 'Dumb Blonde'. Not a collection that I would like to have in my bathroom when visitors were coming! I declined the shampoo treatment, so was just squirted with water instead as my hairdresser snipped and snipped. Her sister appeared and they started having a screaming argument; to my horror my golden locks were falling to the floor with lightning speed. Her temper made her normally sweet face look mean and her voice was harsh and all the time the scissors snipped. The only thing missing was an orchestra rising to a crescendo, the cymbals crashing and me falling dead with scissors stuck in my jugular. I paid my VND 30,000 (£1.50) and fled. I hope Princess Anne appreciates what I have gone through for her reception tomorrow!

So another day when I feel as though I am walking through a stage set and marvel that I am here and it is not a dream. My only wish is that you and Nick and Natasha could be with me. I miss you all so much.

Lots of love, Mum

Hanoi

7 May 2002

Princess Anne is having a reception tonight in the Melia Hotel and the whole world is invited. The office at Save the Children is looking impressive; errant leaves have been swept up, the floors have been mopped and the walls painted. Pictures, photographs, maps, graphs and statistics are on display, and the result is clear, concise and colourful. Her visit has certainly motivated the staff and focused attention on their immediate working environment, and much pride is being taken in the achievements of each individual project. She is visiting us tomorrow. It is also the day that I am visiting a fortune teller.

Today I sat under a tamarind tree and drank coffee. The street still provides as much theatre as anyone could hope to find anywhere. Ladies walk with plastic bags over their heads in order to keep their rollers in place. Hairdressers rush out and hang their yellow-duster-coloured towels on motorbikes to dry before the next customer arrives. Children are constantly being fed from bowls as they explore the pavement, their grannies or mums following behind with a spoon. Tiny charcoal burners provide a livelihood for an entrepreneur as she roasts corn-on-the-cob beside the gutter. I drank my coffee and idly planned what I should wear to the reception tonight.

Tien Yen, 10 May 2002

My dear Gerry and Natasha,

I can't believe this will be my last letter from Tien Yen. So many epistles sent from this room, so many emotions and new impressions that I have tried to share with you. The house is silent at last as everyone has gone to bed. I feel so weepy and I have a sore throat from controlling the tears. We got back from Hanoi yesterday, after driving through some amazing rainstorms. All the coal dust around Cam Pha was washed away and, for the first time since spring, the leaves were green. The new road that normally makes everyone dress like bandits, with kerchiefs over mouths and noses to protect against dust and coal, had flooded and we drove through great lakes of orange water. It must be so soul destroying for the road builders. When we eventually arrived in our little town, everything was damp and fresh and everyone was out in the evening sun.

Today has been sleepy and quiet. More rain, so Xuan and I have talked and talked. We have been making up for all the long intervals when we have been apart, through training or visitors or just mood swings. We talk about books we want to read and about films and hobbies that we want to see or do together, then we remember that our way of life is about to change and she will say, 'Oh, of course we can't.'

We only have one more week together before she leaves for a training course. I shall then stay on for the last week with Thau. We'll continue to be friends in Hanoi, though we won't see that much of each other, and Xuan is as excited as me about my new apartment. Mr Trinh has promised to bring me crabs and prawns and oranges from Tien Yen, and we have hopes to continue the liaison with our ethnic teachers. Anything is possible.

I know that I do not want to stay longer but, as I sit in this room that has seen so much happen, I know that I shall miss it all. We laugh as we remember the training sessions, the singing of Santa Lucia, decorating the office and the continual sewing of the quilt. So many nights when Xuan patiently tried to teach me computer skills, or worked out patterns for the quilt for me in various colours and designs. We reminisce about how we used to suddenly get inspired and start serious planning for the coming month or the next school visits at odd times, like late Friday afternoon when the rest of the world was clocking off and going home.

We both look at the box that we used to block the hole under the stairs where Mr Darcy liked to hoard the smelly treasures he found on his walks; neither of us have had the heart to move it.

I was invited to a huge reception for the Queen's Jubilee, so was one of the thousand who mingled with 'the great and the good'. It was wonderful; I wore my black ao dai, ate smoked salmon, drank wine and ate Stilton and cheddar cheese and Walkers crisps that had all been specially flown in! Not my usual night in Hanoi, that is for sure.

The following morning we all gathered at the SCF office and waited for the 'royal visit'. Princess Anne was everything she was cracked up to be. She was knowledgeable, committed and probably knew more about our projects than any one as; after all, she has been Patron for Save the Children since 1970. Two ethnic teachers had travelled down to Hanoi for the visit; they looked so colourful in their Dau and San Chi clothes, and were so very self-contained and dignified as they met Her Royal Highness. Princess Anne was charming to all of us, and she spoke to me in detail about teaching methods and how young children learn through play and pictures. There was a general discussion about Bich's plan to raise rabbits for food, and when I told her about the flopsy bunnies she made a face and squeezed my hand.

I am still feeling quite low key; I suppose it must be the rain. On a positive note, the labyrinthitis seems to be getting a little better, although the headaches are worse, on the left hand side, above my ear.

I really like my new apartment. I am also looking forward to going to visit Clare in her National Park and then on to Hoi An for the VSO conference.

All for now,
Love Mum

Tien Yen
13 May 2002

Xuan and I have been studying the paper that I got from the fortune teller. I still smile when I think of the night that we went to see him. We had Princess Anne's visit in the morning and then the fortune teller in the evening. His house was in a part of Hanoi that I had never visited before, and we had to weave through a maze of alleyways on Xuan's motorbike to get there. As we arrived clouds were billowing in shades of dark greys to ominous thundery black and great fat drops of rain had started to fall. She wheeled her bike into his sitting room but, naturally, we left our shoes at the door.

The room was small; we sat on the sofa and the fortune teller sat across from us with all his exercise books laid out in front of him on the coffee table. He was in his fifties, reminding me of a college professor somehow, and he was in no hurry as he drew my chart in blue and red ink. It was very important to have the exact time of birth apparently, as well as the date, and from this he then did some complicated sums. Xuan and I sat for two hours as he told me about my past, my children, my parents and my divorce. He even told me about my back operation.

Then he told me about my having just acquired a new place to live in Vietnam and about leaving Tien Yen. He charted the years that I would have money and seemed to think I might live to be quite old, and then he told me I would marry again, next year!

It is so silly, I know…

Here in Tien Yen the rain continues, the river has burst its banks and we have heard that a huge bridge near Binh Lieu has collapsed and will take a month or so to fix. There is little for us to do as the roads are totally impassable. We sit in the house listening to the rain on the iron roofs, and everything is damp.

Tien Yen, 20 May 2002

My dear Gerry and Natasha,

It is my last day and it is raining and I have spent most of the morning curled up with a hangover, feeling vulnerable and terrified of confronting all the people that I kissed last night. SCF and the District Education Department gave me the most fantastic farewell party. The speeches, presents and food were all out of this world. Hang made every single one of my favourite dishes and I drank the equivalent of a small loch. I had everyone at the table balancing bottles and glasses on their heads, and then I conducted renditions of all my favourite Vietnamese songs. People in the street outside stopped to listen; maybe they thought we were a choir practicing. Later there was karaoke (of course) and I vaguely remember walking home, probably still singing.

The Director of Education is in Hanoi at the moment, but he rang during all this nonsense to say goodbye. I remember inviting him round to my new house in Hang Gai Street. Oh God! So yes, it is now a time for quiet, Ibuprofen and packing. Somehow I don't feel too sad. Hanoi isn't so far away; these farewells only mark a change in lifestyle, and I have made some very warm and wonderful friends. I have lots to look forward to, a new job and a new home. My new kitchen is red and is dominated by a giant poster of Ho Chi Minh, the study/bedroom has a giant dance mirror, and the balcony is overflowing with plants and ferns and trees. I think it will all be fine.

Remember my first visit to this house in Tien Yen? I remember writing about the sinking feeling I had when I first saw my room. The bareness, the lonely light bulb, the shared toilet facilities, the close living proximity, the bats and the spider. I felt as though I had stepped into a scene from The Inn of the Sixth Happiness, except that this is rural Vietnam, not China. We now have a huge rat as well as the bats.

I have had so many children and teachers share my life, I just hope that the experience has given my sense of values a jolt. I know I won't take so many things for granted anymore. Just a normal two-way conversation might be nice – that is, without a translator!

I have been trying to pack and I cannot believe the rubbish I have collected. Nothing will fit into my suitcases and I shall look like some wandering peasant woman with my army of plastic bags. Oh the shame.

I have requested my ticket to be brought forward. All this rain has brought down bridges and washed away the almost non-existent roads, so it's pointless staying on. So get the vacuum cleaner out and please email me about the weather. Here it is now 33°C and so sticky; our clothes are wet and Xuan has her hair all pinned up like a Japanese Geisha. The rain falls directly into Hang's kitchen area, it is all so damp and humid and only the fan is constant as the noises of the street are punctuated by sloshing car tyres and the slip-slop sound of sandals as people rush past.

It is a 'family' dinner tonight and then I'm off early in the morning. I cannot believe it is for the last time.

See you very soon,

Love Mum

Edinburgh
26 June 2002

It is a rainy afternoon in Edinburgh. My white rose bush is being battered against the window, people are dressed in their best black raincoats and all the shop windows are exposing bodies in very little. It would appear to be summer everywhere except here.

I have been back in Scotland for almost four weeks and have criss-crossed the country, gazing at fields and orderly traffic lanes, from Skye to Dundee, Perth to Glencoe. I have listened to stories about people that I know and used to know, and have just loved watching friends' faces and hearing their voices. I have fallen into the holiday mode of not being sure what day it is and, better still, not caring.

I have had my photos developed. I stood on the clean, wide, uncluttered pavement and stared at images of Bac Ma National Park in Vietnam. It was a former hill station used by the French in their colonial era, about forty minutes south of Hue.

I looked at the photographs and suddenly I was thousands of miles away, listening to Clare telling me about the use of the summit as a helicopter base during the Vietnam War and how the Vietcong had burrowed caves into the hillsides and conducted their own sort of warfare amongst the thick natural jungle. There were so many dead that, even now, people say they can hear the voices of spirits in the wind, men who were not buried according to tradition and so are not able to join their ancestors.

The day I climbed to the summit was hot and steamy. I explored the waterfall trail ('DO NOT STRAY OFF PATHS, UNEXPLODED MINES') and I climbed down the six hundred and ninety steps to the foot of the waterfall ('DO NOT

ATTEMPT IF YOU ARE NOT FIT'). I stared at the amazing deluge, not noticing the coiled green snake so close and alert and watching me. I was about to take a photograph, and it was only as I lowered my camera in order to judge the shot that I saw what was just about a metre from my feet. I suddenly felt fragile and vulnerable and very alone. I retreated and, as I tried to climb back up, my heart and lungs were just about exploding, sweat soaked my clothes and I had to stop every few minutes in order to pull leeches off my ankles and try to breath again.

It was funny flicking through photos and seeing images of myself leaning against a palm tree on a beach en route to a VSO conference in Hoi An. The whole day suddenly comes back and Edinburgh disappears and I can feel again the sand on my feet and that first taste of 7-Up when I was dying of thirst.

Hoi An was the most beautiful town I saw in Vietnam. I only saw it once in daylight, that first afternoon when we arrived and hired bicycles to ride to the sea. The conference started early in the morning and finished after the sun had set, so we wandered through the darkening streets like alley cats, drinking gin and tonics at happy hour, glasses lined up in front of us as we didn't want to drink doubles. The streets at night were beautiful, the buildings and architecture very Chinese. Hoi An was, in fact, the site of the first Chinese settlement in southern Vietnam, and parts of the town look exactly the same as they might have done a hundred and fifty years ago. We cruised, looking at shops selling delicate, peaceful Vietnamese paintings, contrasting with about two hundred tailor shops frantically running up suits and dresses for clients to pick up within a day of ordering. In all this frenzy we walked about, woozy and full of gin, feeling as though we were on a film set...

As I stood on the wet Scottish pavement, I smiled at the pictures of Clare and Emma in My Son, the remains of an old Hindu-style (Cham) temple settlement dating from the tenth century. It was very Indiana Jones and we searched for all the focal points indicated in the Lonely Planet. We saw where the B52 bombers had destroyed some parts and where the jungle had re-seeded itself in between the ancient stonework, causing great chunks to fall as the new plants came to life and split the stones with their great python-like roots.

It had been so hot and silent. We made our own tableau, surrounded by the mountains, trees and the lost settlement, and I was reminded of Keats. In a dusty classroom long ago I read 'Ode on a Grecian Urn' and pictured the scene of a young man spending eternity in pursuit of his love. He would never catch her, he would never know the joys of fulfilment or disillusionment. It was left for the reader to imagine, and similarly we made our own picture on that sultry afternoon. It was a moment frozen in time, and we three would never be the same again. Our lives had been joined by our volunteer experience and it had brought us together in a clearing, alone, in the centre of Vietnam. Soon we would part and only these photographs would remind me of Clare's voice and Emma's laugh and my red dress.

The return to Hanoi was long; fifteen hours on a 'soft' sleeper. I shared with three men and watched with horror as the one opposite my bunk clipped his toenails. He then produced a long, thin stick, like an incense stick with a fluffy end which you might clean a keyboard with, and stuck it in his ear. All this while the train rocked about. They slurped noodles, played loud music, and then eventually settled down and snored. I studiously avoided all eye contact and read, then slept huddled under my sheet fully clothed. When we parted in Hanoi at five in the morning they were polite and considerate and we all shook hands as though we were lifelong friends.

I don't have the photos yet of my last trip to the Chua

Thay Pagoda, about an hour and a half from Hanoi. Richard took me to the loveliest little village, almost medieval with its warren of streets. Everything was dominated by the rice harvest and the smell of cut hay was strong as we walked over the drying sheaves and husks scattered over the roads. The sun was hot, we were dripping with perspiration and the village seemed to be bathed in a yellow glow.

We climbed the steep steps up to the pagoda, which had been carved into the side of the mountain. We visited and prayed and lit about fifty incense sticks, photographed a seven hundred-year-old frangipani tree and felt as though we were intruding. The day before a much-loved monk had died, so people were sitting in front of his blown up picture and the altar was covered in fruit and offerings. The mourners had yellow bandanas on, the sign of grieving for a holy man.

Richard was horrified that we were asked to sign a book after we had donated our small notes into a collection box for money to refurbish the roof. I think we were ashamed that if there was no other money in the box, then they would know how little we had given. It made us feel so mean, though we did buy lots of water, bracelets and a pretty fan.

The temple was amazing and very unusual as the Buddhas and statues were all as black as ebony and decorated in silver.

We were ushered out and told to follow the path that led ever upwards. The sun was so high in the sky that the heat made every step feel excruciating as we climbed up the side of the mountain. It was bliss to enter the shady recess at the top, and from there we descended into a cave, totally in darkness except for the feeble light from the torch we had hired. Silly white tape was the only deterrent against our falling to our deaths, and a skull and cross bones had been drawn on the wall to warn us of the danger. The cave was like a yawning black hole, its size giving the illusion of an underground cathedral. Steps had been cut into the ground, making progress a little easier, but no less precarious, as our eyes strained in the gloom for the next step amongst the ooze and slime. The damp air dripped down the ancient walls and every surface was wet and slippery. After we had walked far into the cave we were suddenly bathed in white light coming from a natural fissure in the rock high above us. We were mere ants at the bottom of the vast cavern and the sun fell like a shimmery curtain around us. We half expected to see a giant opera singer or fragile ballet dancer take to the spotlight. Instead, Richard took a picture of me, sporting the Vietnamese flag on my red T-shirt...

It is strange thinking of it now, from Edinburgh's chilly, windswept streets, and recalling how hot and humid we were that day. It was just so perfect to emerge into the sunlight and look down onto the patchwork of rice fields. A whole spectrum of green spread out below us, from watery silver through to the deepest emerald. We made our way down and, if I close my eyes now, I can see Richard amongst a group of laughing children as he picked up a little yellow duckling from the dusty road and stood smiling... it was an almost perfect picture that encompasses that whole perfect day.

We gazed at the poplars forming avenues and we had to blink and wonder if we really were in Vietnam, but the sight of the old woman at the well in her conical hat, the grinning boys swimming in the lotus pond and the waiting 'Honda Dream' motorbike made us smile. We knew that we couldn't be anywhere else.

Balcony, Hang Gai Street, Hanoi
July 2002

The plane dipped in its descent towards Hanoi, sweeping low over green-forested mountains. The clouds cleared and suddenly I could see Ba Vi National Park looming tall out of the mists, every road and track so familiar. The beautiful Red River valley lay beneath, as it had on the day that I had stood at the top of the mountain, gazing down from the great heights where the pagodas had been built.

Richard had stridden ahead, shouting as leeches circled his ankles like black bracelets, and we had stopped as he prised them off. That day they were more discerning; they must have preferred the higher alcohol level in his blood, as they didn't touch me.

I gazed down and I was back with Richard, exploring every inch of the National Park. The motorbike took us along countless tracks darkened by the luxuriant jungle growth, and we got off to watch dung beetles patiently go to work on their midday meal. We saw long black worms almost half a metre long, and a lost village that had once been a mountain retreat for the French.

There had once been bungalows set amidst beautifully landscaped gardens. A church with gothic windows was set back from the road and we had tentatively explored, afraid of the snakes that undoubtedly lurked amidst the damp dark stones and overgrown grasses. Even though it had no roof, there was a stillness and quiet that time had not destroyed.

The jungle had reclaimed the village, leaving a scene that could evoke nightmares. One house had literally been strangled by long white penetrating roots. The brickwork had crumbled and it needed little imagination to conjure up a living Triffid-like force. We walked into the hushed quiet of another ruin and found a giant taproot forcing its way down, almost like the central column that might uphold the construction instead of being the force of destruction. We wondered about the families that might have lived there and tried to imagine their lives and hopes and dreams. We stood and looked and were saddened by the obvious mortality of our own very existence.

Ba Vi saw us play with seven black bears that had been rescued from the hunter's traps; the baby bear was tame enough to lick honey from our fingers. Later we ate with the Forest Rangers during a huge tropical storm, but didn't realise until afterwards that one of the dishes was dog. Richard ate heartily although he was quite anaesthetised by the local rice wine, which he and the rangers had been drinking very competitively.

As my plane flew over the now-familiar shape of the two peaks, I saw the white strip of the road meandering over the hillside and I remembered it all. The pagoda was set high on top of the mountain, so we had to climb almost vertically through deep forest. We then staggered up the seemingly endless concrete steps, gasping for breath, whilst our sweat just ran like rivers, soaking Richard's shirt and running down my neck and collecting in pools in my bra. The humidity hung in the air and all was silent except for our footsteps through the leaves and undergrowth. On reaching the top we lay down on two hard stone benches and gazed up through the branches of a flame tree, its feathery fronds and scarlet blossoms providing shade from the midday sun. Once we had recovered, we tried to capture the view of the whole valley through the lenses of our cameras. The panorama just swept beneath us, the great lazy river with the buffaloes and farm scenes, and, in the distance, the chain of misty blue, rugged peaks, rising into the bluest of skies. Pictures could not capture the silence and the heat, Richard's laugh, or my feeling that I might die of thirst. All of these memories would be triggered later when I looked at the photographs.

Inside the pagoda, the altar was laden with offerings of fruit and flowers and incense sticks. The aura was hushed and still; only the cicadas disturbed the peace. We took off our shoes and went inside. As we approached the Buddha, we found that the face representing love and a quest for a better way to live one's life was not actually the one normally associated with Buddha, but, in fact, was a bust of Ho Chi Minh. The great man certainly is a focus for love and veneration and patriotic unity, but I wonder how he would feel, knowing that he is being worshipped so openly.

The hill station was beautiful, especially since there were so few tourists there and we were able to explore alone. We swam in a pool which could have been cleaner, ate spinach, fish, soup and rice, and drank the inevitable Vietnamese vodka. We told each other stories, sang songs, and went for walks in the forest, serenaded by the noises of cicadas and insects. The night was black, lit only by half a moon and a million stars...

I was bumped back into reality as the plane landed. My new life was about to begin. I was determined to be optimistic. I was excited by the familiar road chaos and smells, and the colour and vibrancy that met my eyes as the taxi drew into the heart of the city. I knew I wanted to be here in Hanoi and that the lessons I had learned from the people whose lives I had shared so intimately had changed me. I am still searching for answers and I am still an incurable romantic, but I do believe that there is a rough justice in this cosmos of ours. Pain inflicted will come back like a boomerang, and the months spent in Tien Yen helped me to reflect on the decisions I had made in the past and the reasons behind them. Long ago in Glenelg, my neighbour Mary told me that you should never gloat on another's mistakes or misfortunes, for as sure as death the banana skin would be waiting for you or yours around the next corner.

Richard helped me move my things into Hang Gai Street and together we set the baby trees on the balcony. He kissed me goodbye and wished me well.

Balcony, Hang Gai Street, Hanoi

August 2002

When I look at my quilt, I shall always see the greens of the rice fields of Vietnam. When I look at the threads I used to stitch it, they seem to represent the silver tears and golden memories that I shared with Richard.

Life will go on, but I know now that I can cope alone.

I have been homesick since I got back to Hanoi, which is only natural, but I have been getting reacquainted with all my markets and shops and eating places, and Xuan has rung and told me all the news of Tien Yen. Mr Trinh had arrived in the car with five hundred white rabbits. He had left them in the office in the care of Hang, then went back to collect Xuan and Hiep. Hang discovered that about two hundred of the rabbits had got out and were hopping about all over the place and she couldn't catch them. By the time Xuan arrived they were still bouncing about in my old bedroom and under the stairs. I presume this week will see the distribution of the bunnies.

For me, the new school term begins next week so I have some time to get settled before I start.

I sometimes ache for Scotland and a way of life that I know and understand. I long for the great solid shapes of the mountains around Kintail, the silence and the moonlight on the empty road as it snakes over the Bealach on Mam Ratagan. I can almost hear the waves sploshing on the rounded boulders all covered in whelks and slimy weed, and hear the cry of the gulls as they soar over the windswept beaches on the Isle of Skye. Then I look up to the stars here in Hanoi and see the moon, huge and silver and nestling in the branches of the banyan tree. I know it is not time to go home yet.

Printed in the United States
52147LVS00001B/38